Thank you for your purchase! If you are satisfied with your purchase, please consider leaving a review. It takes 5 seconds and greatly helps out small busninesses like ours.

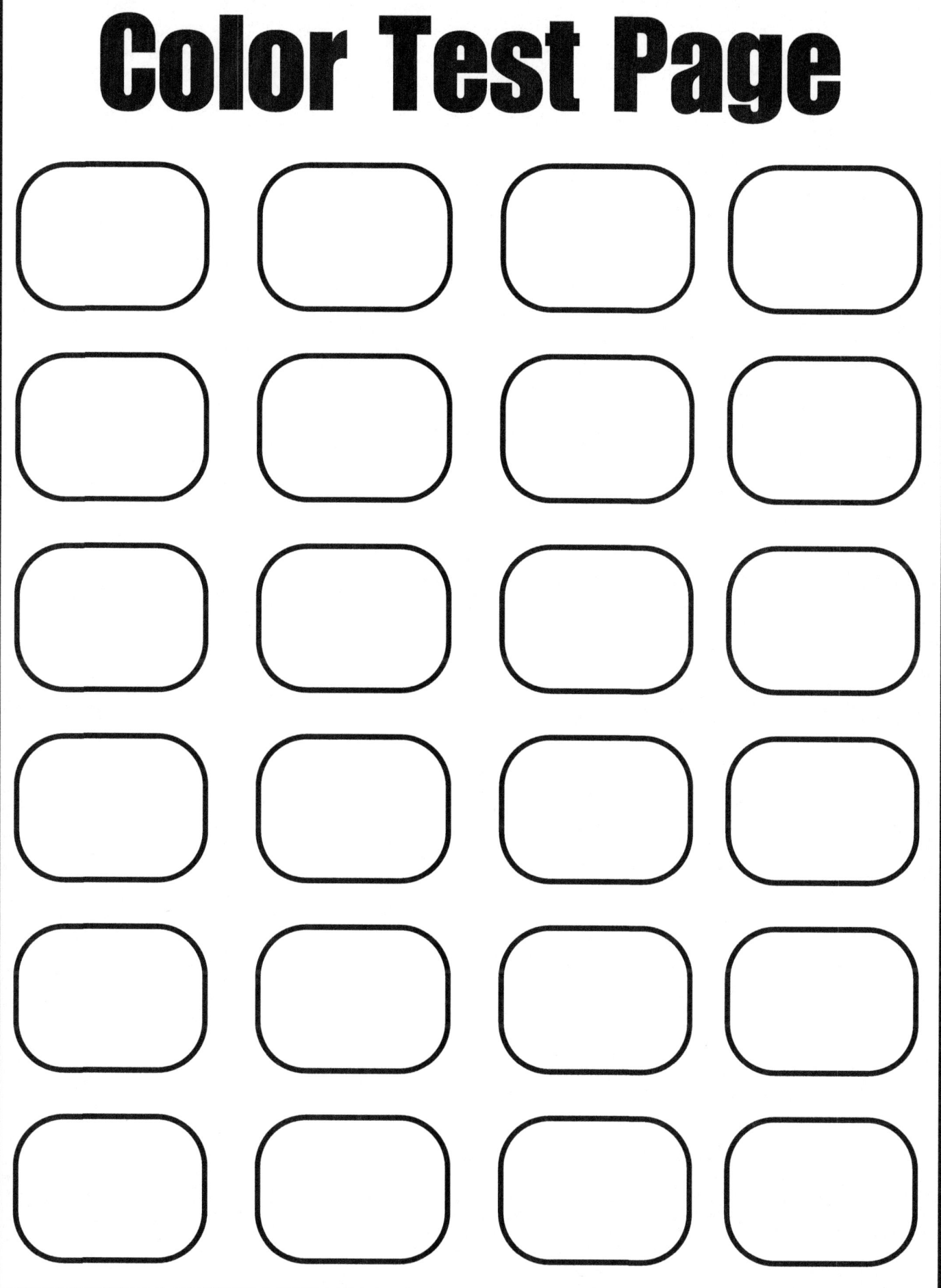

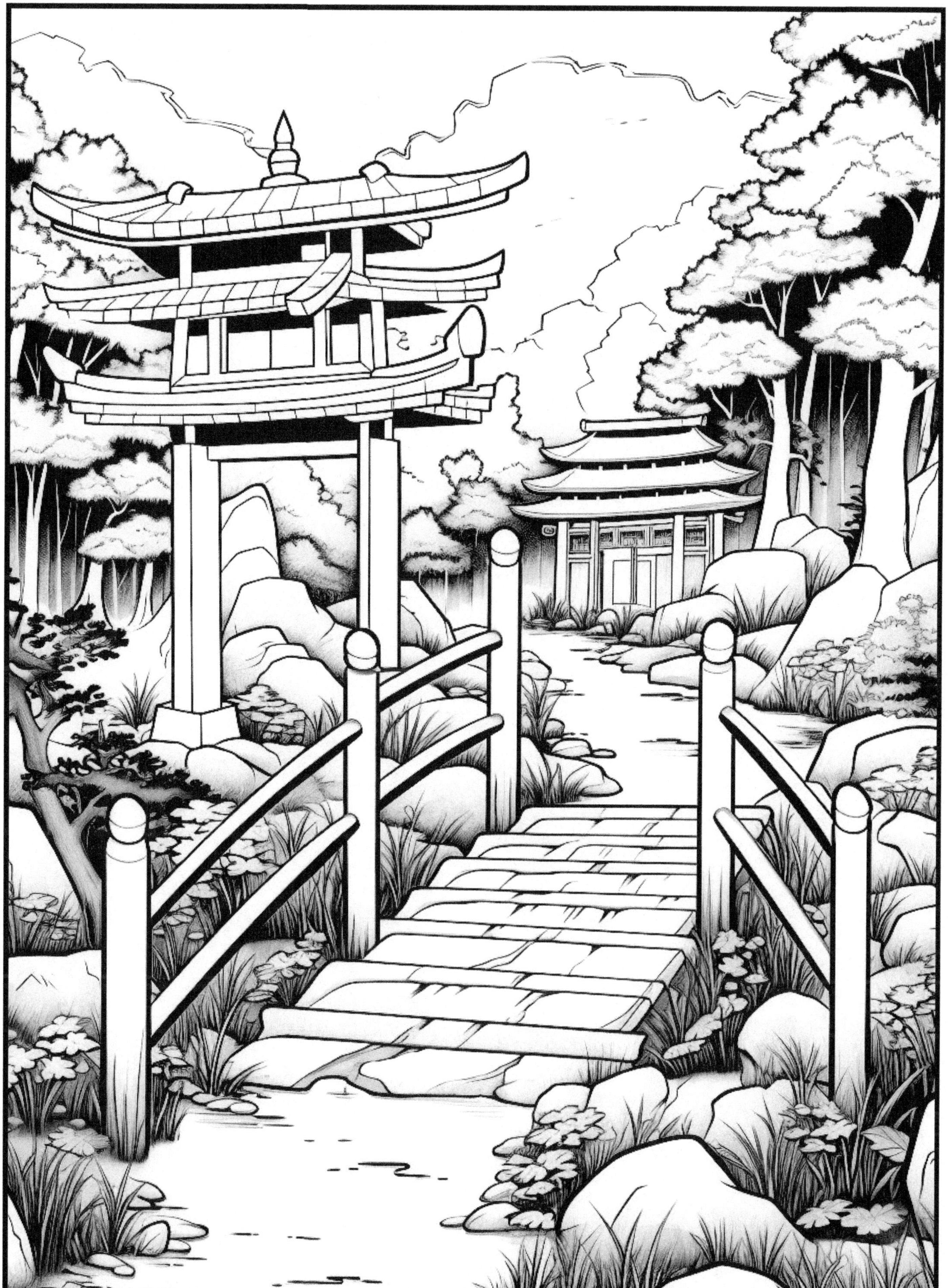

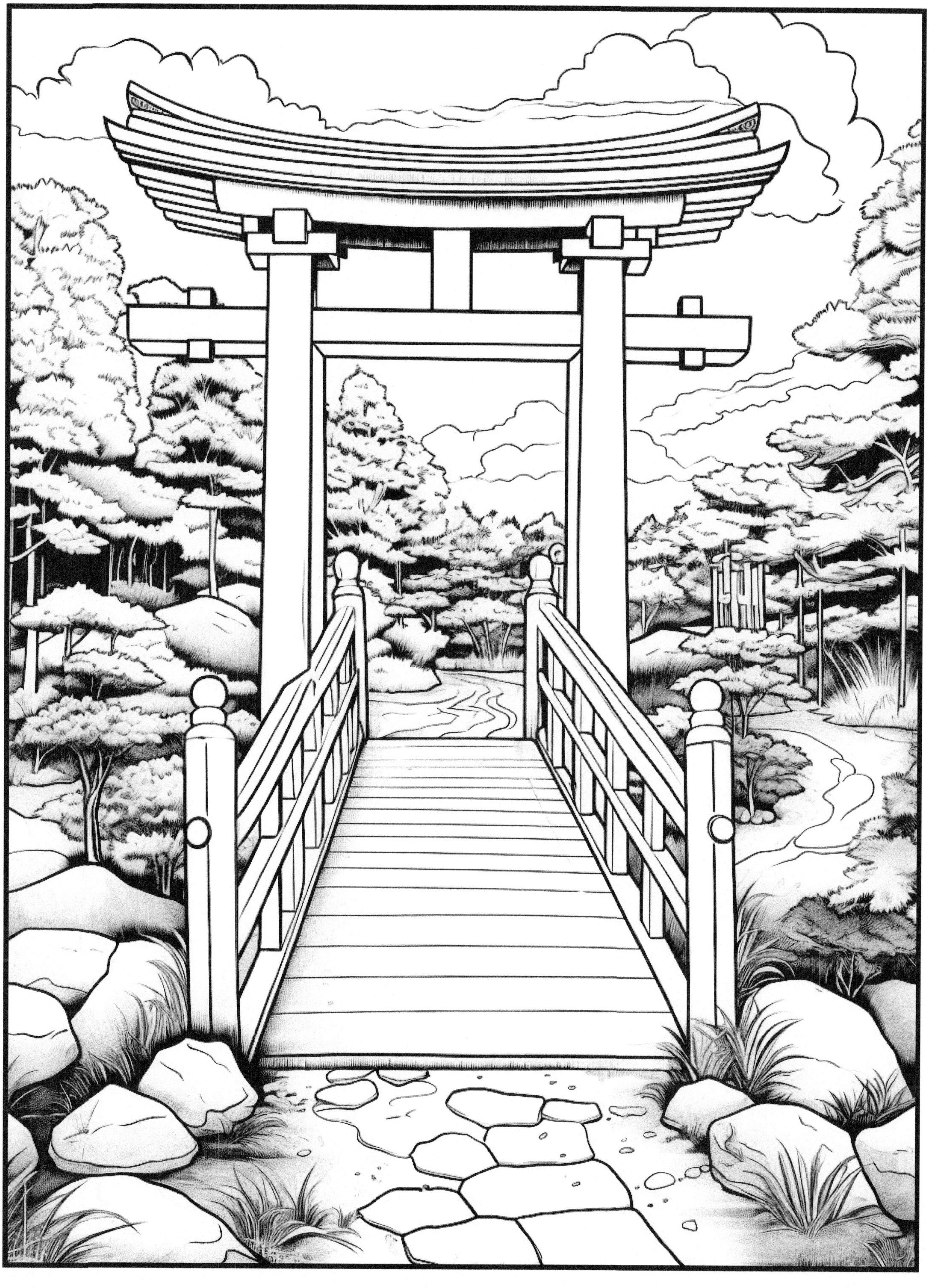

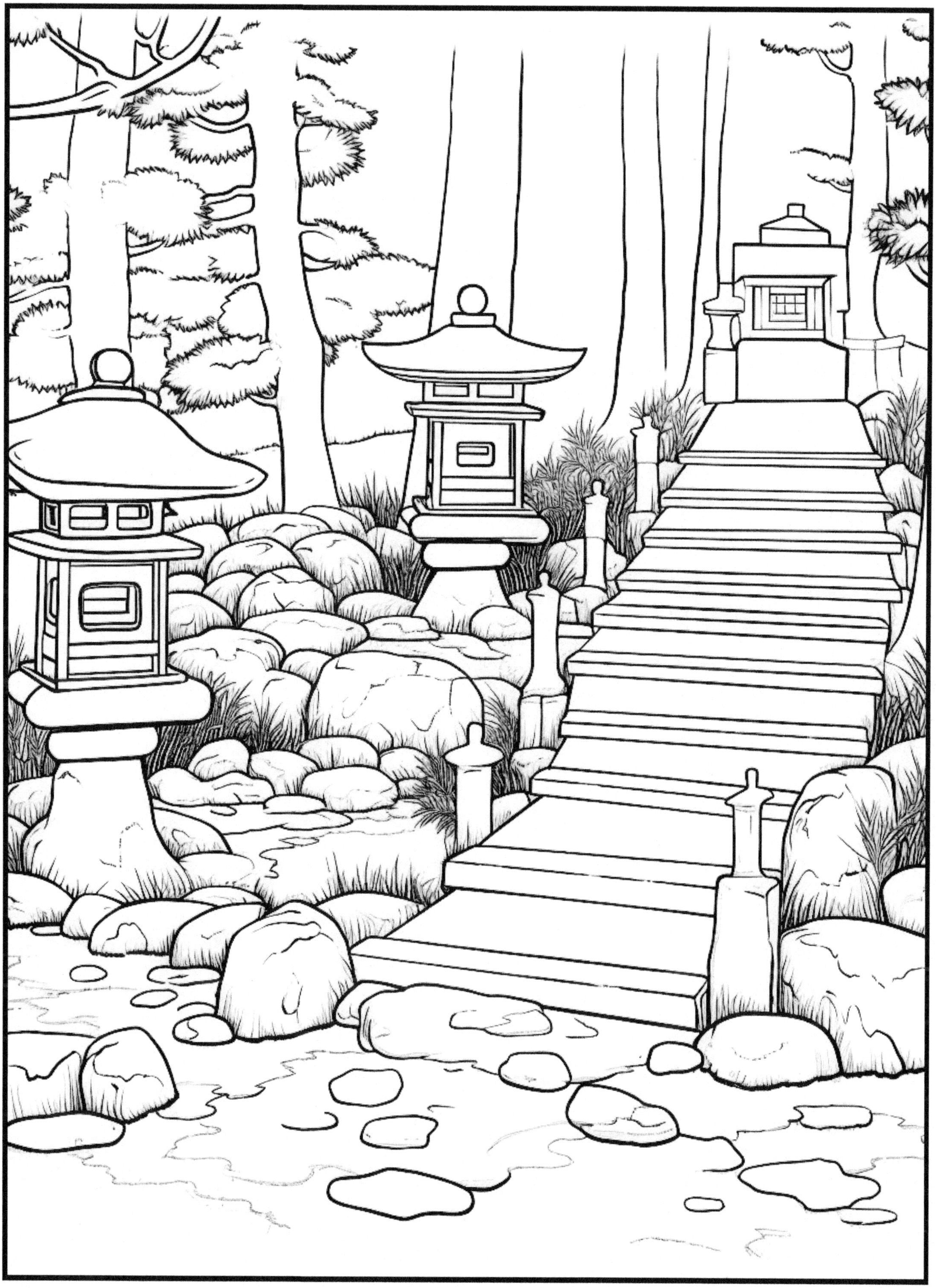

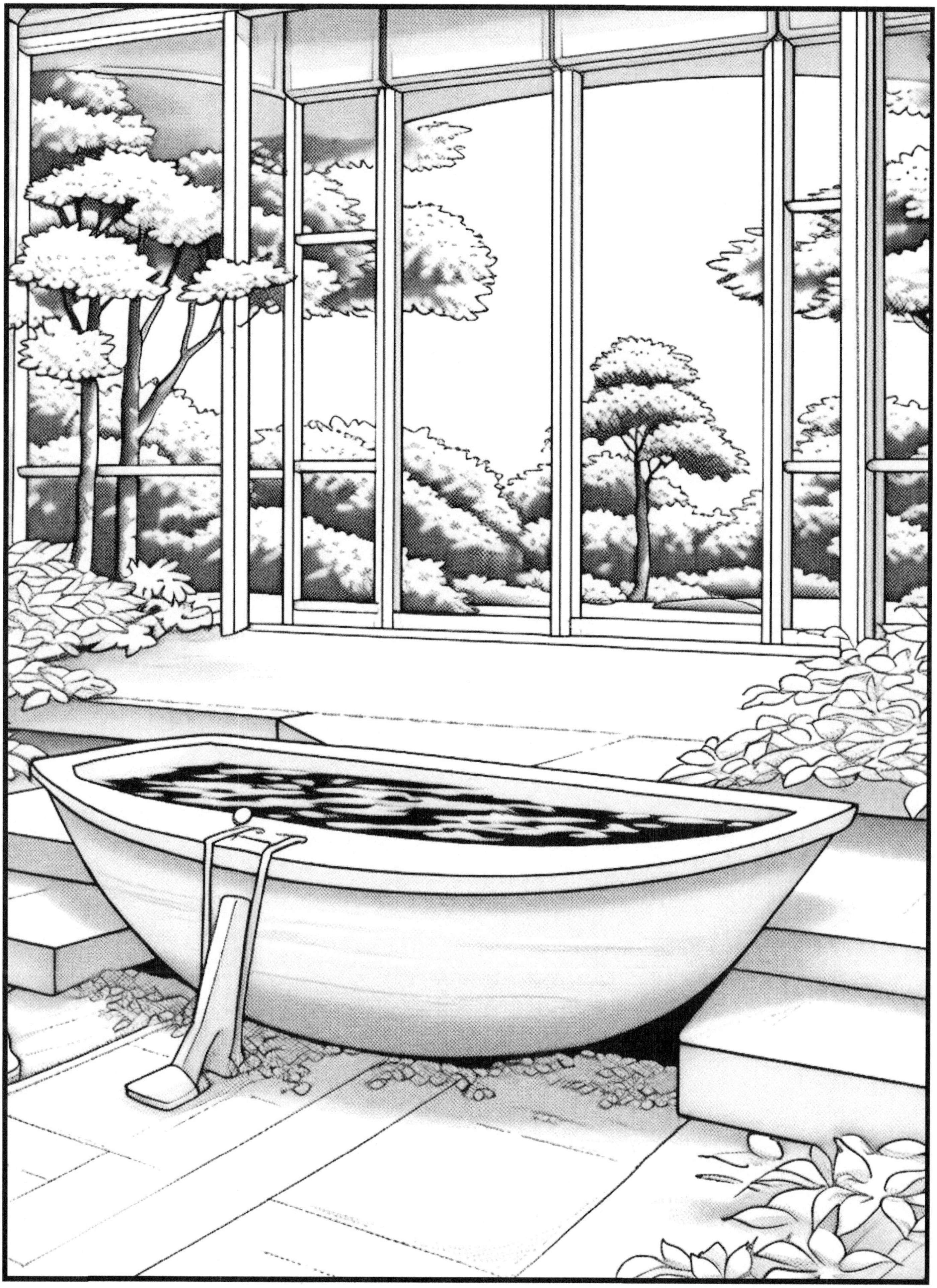

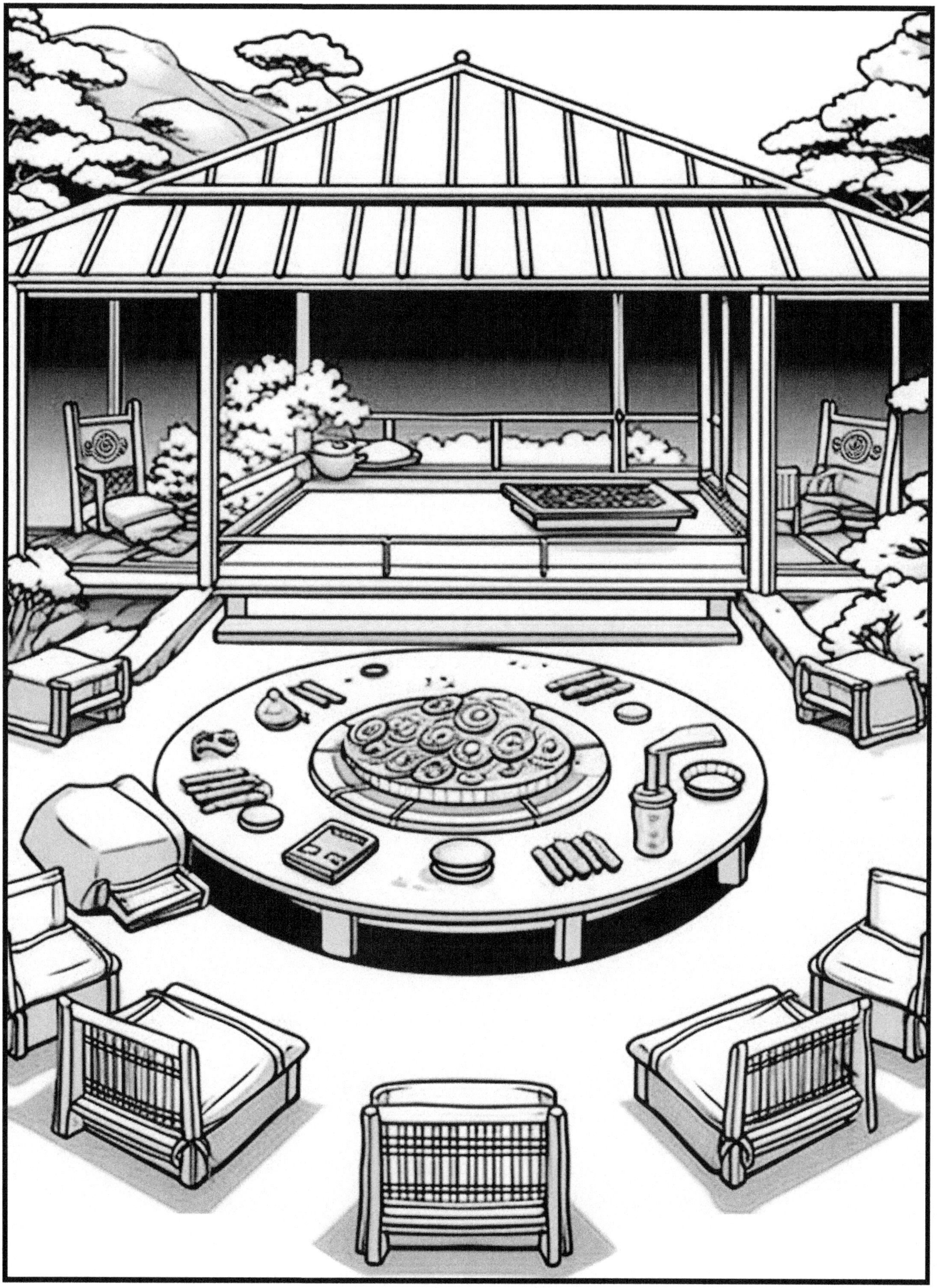

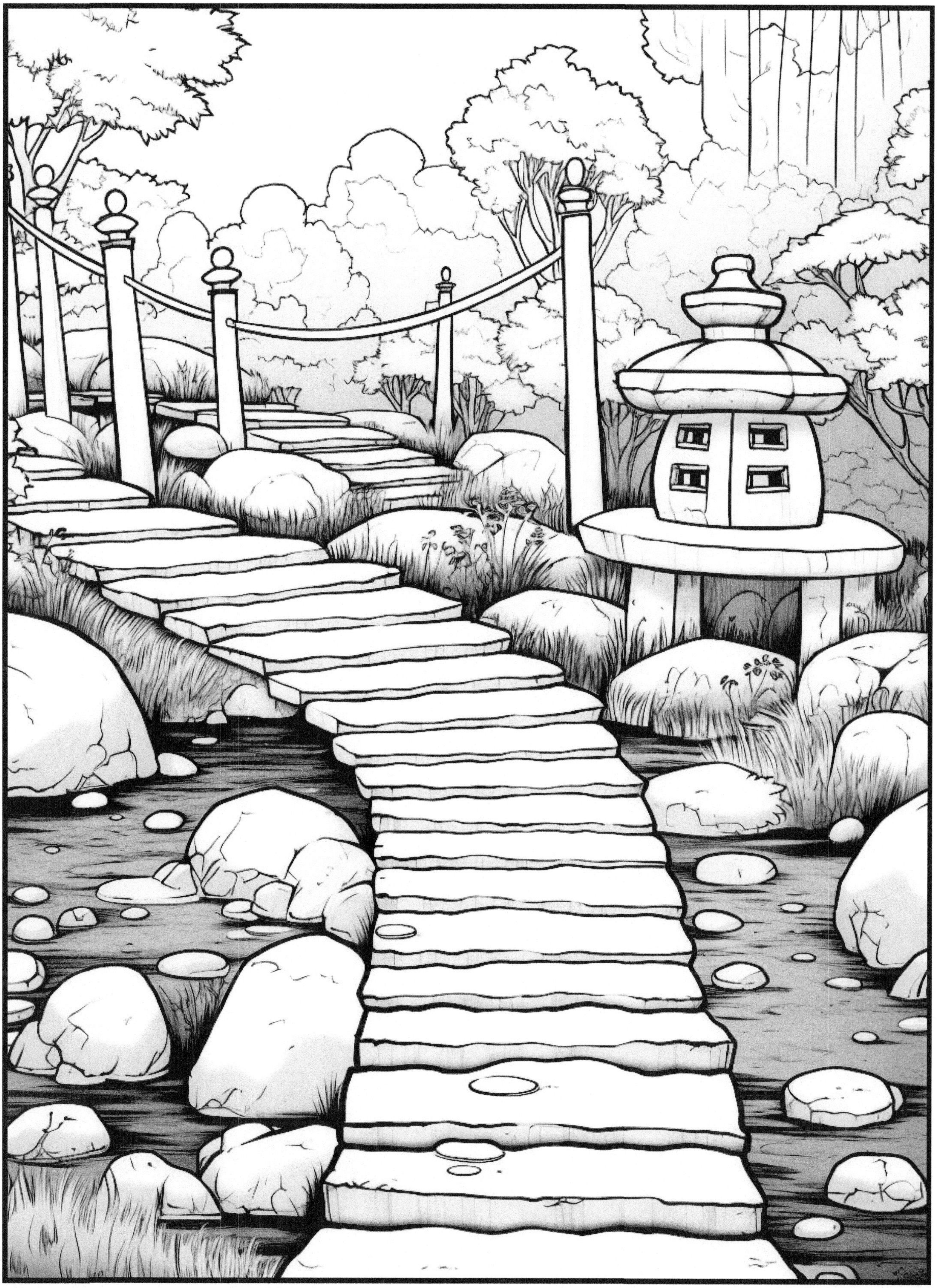

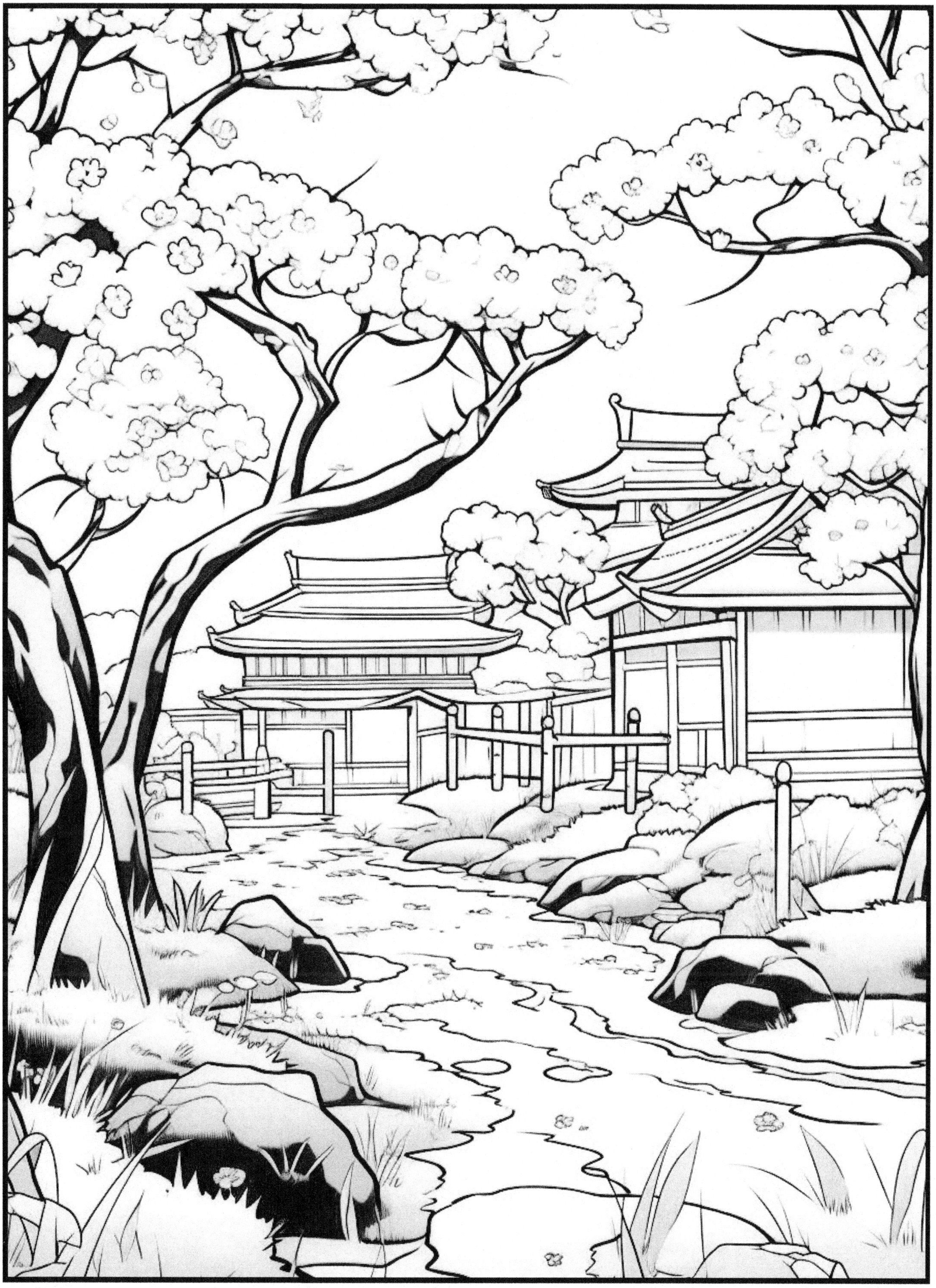

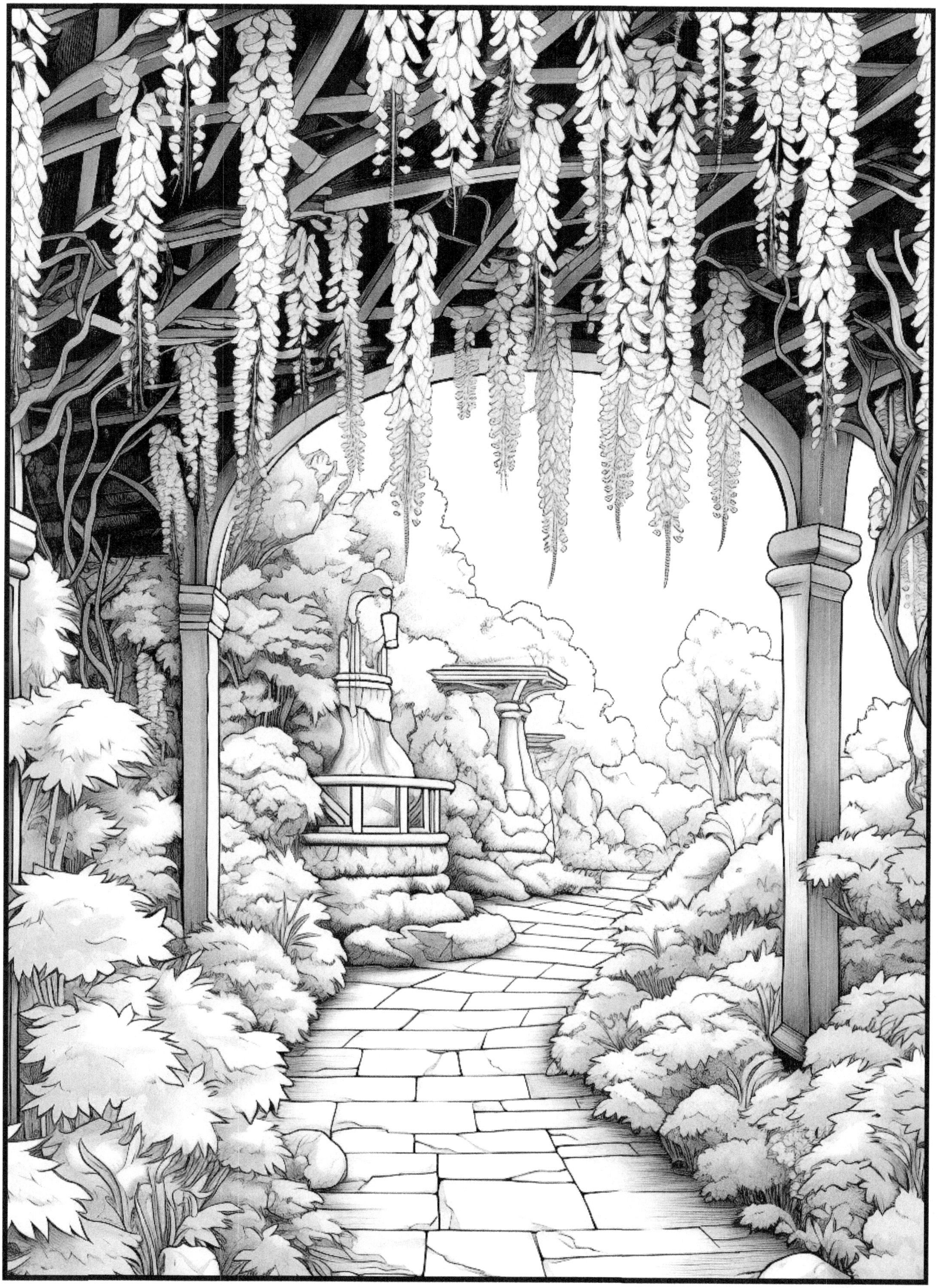

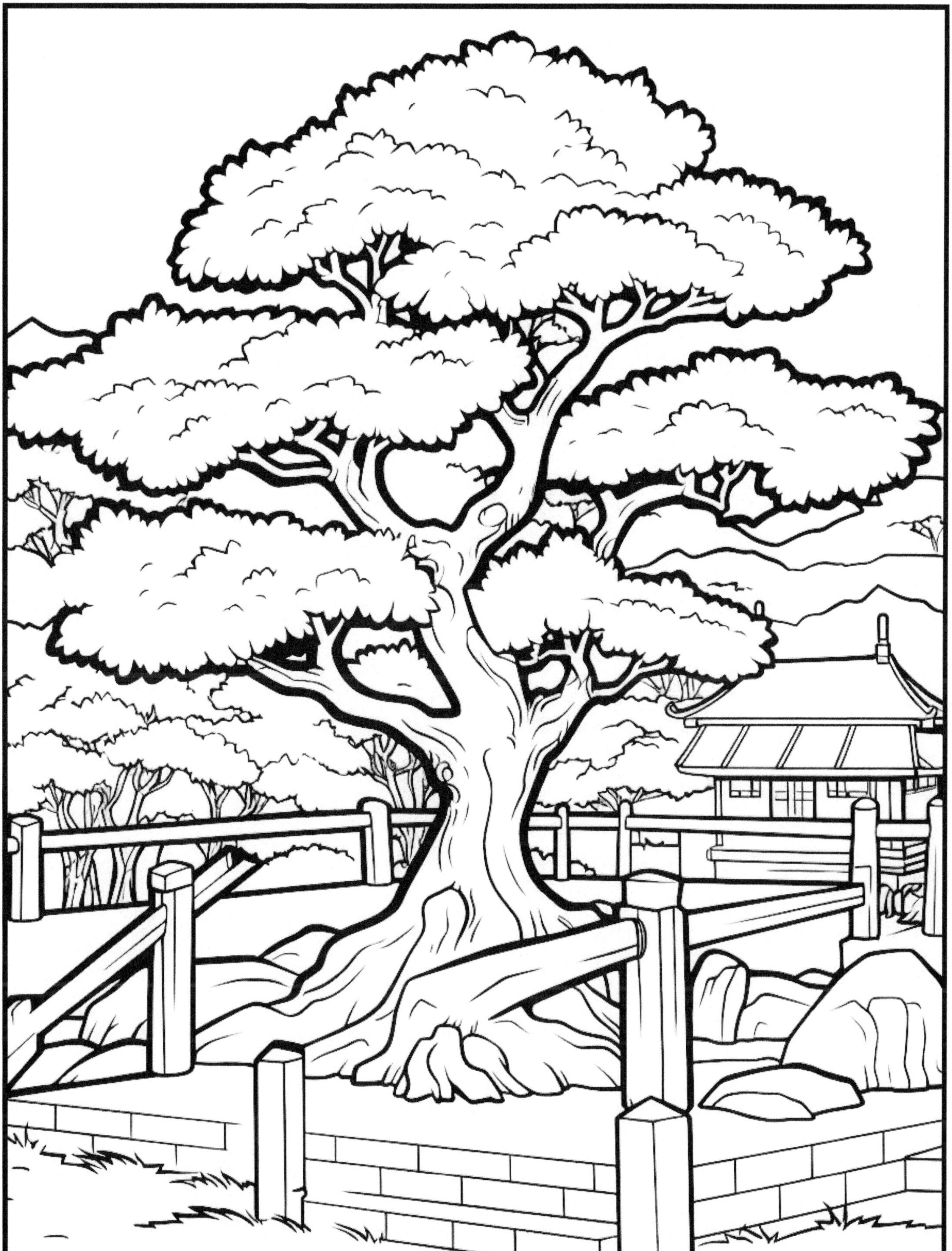

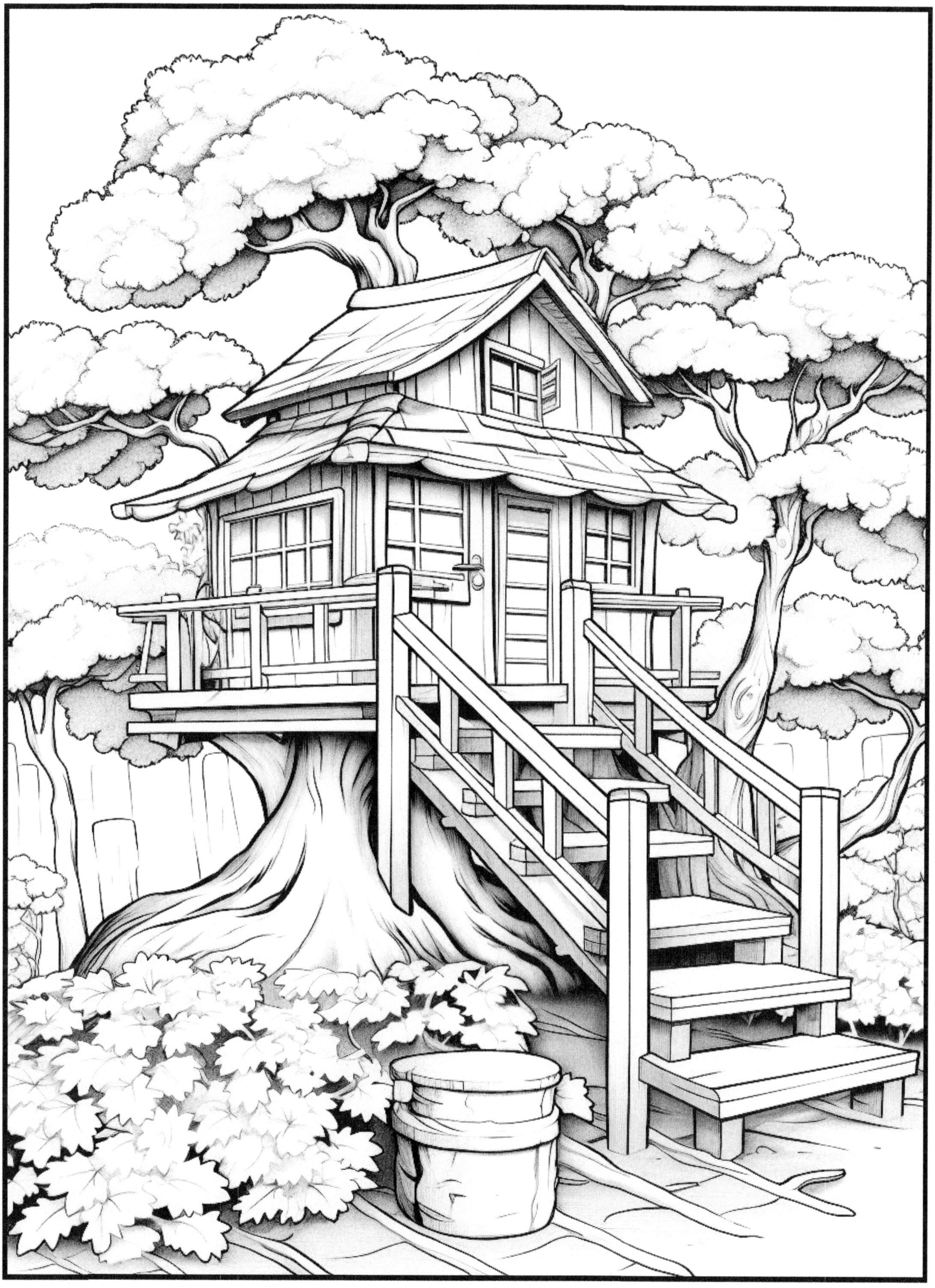

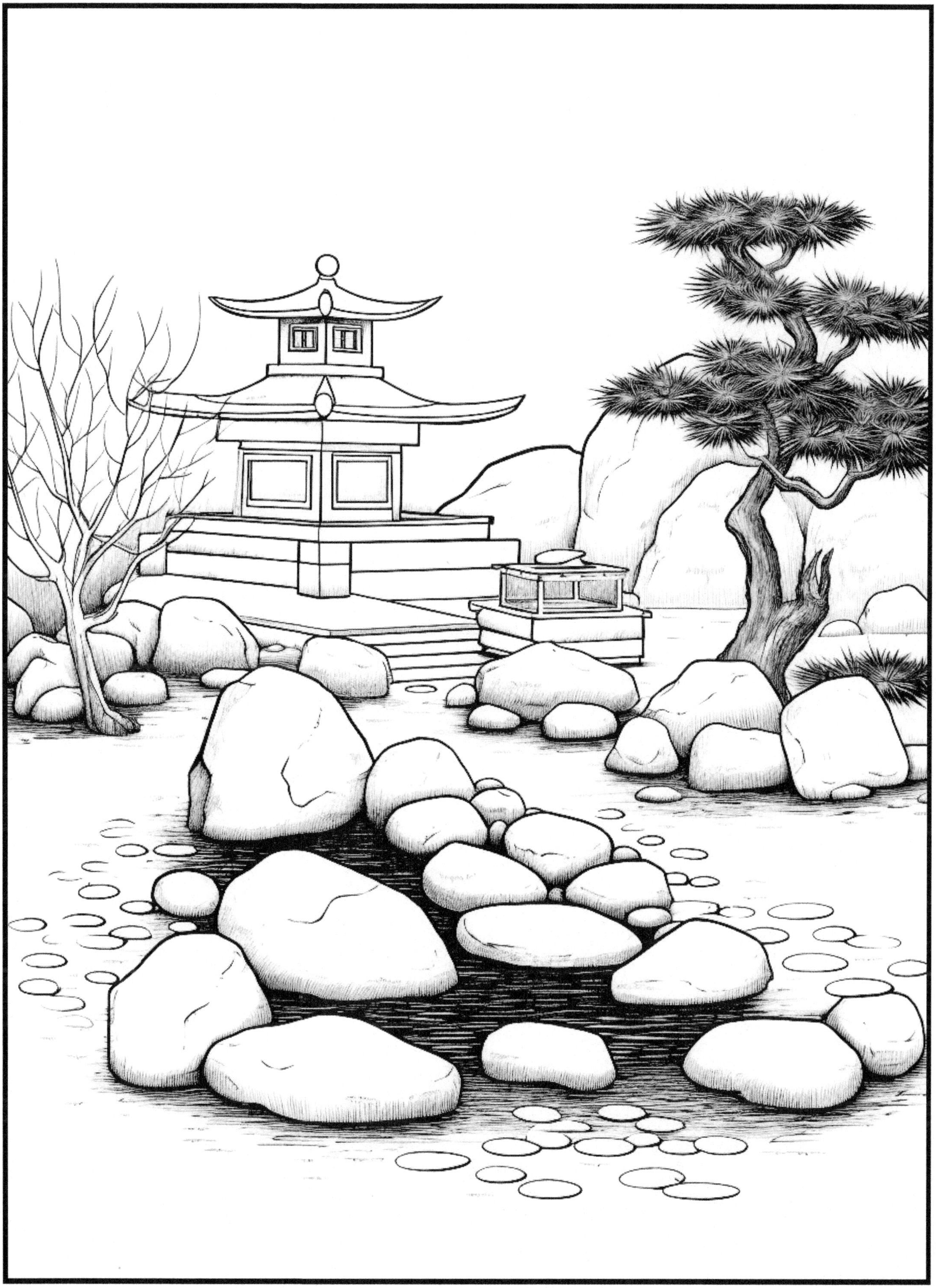

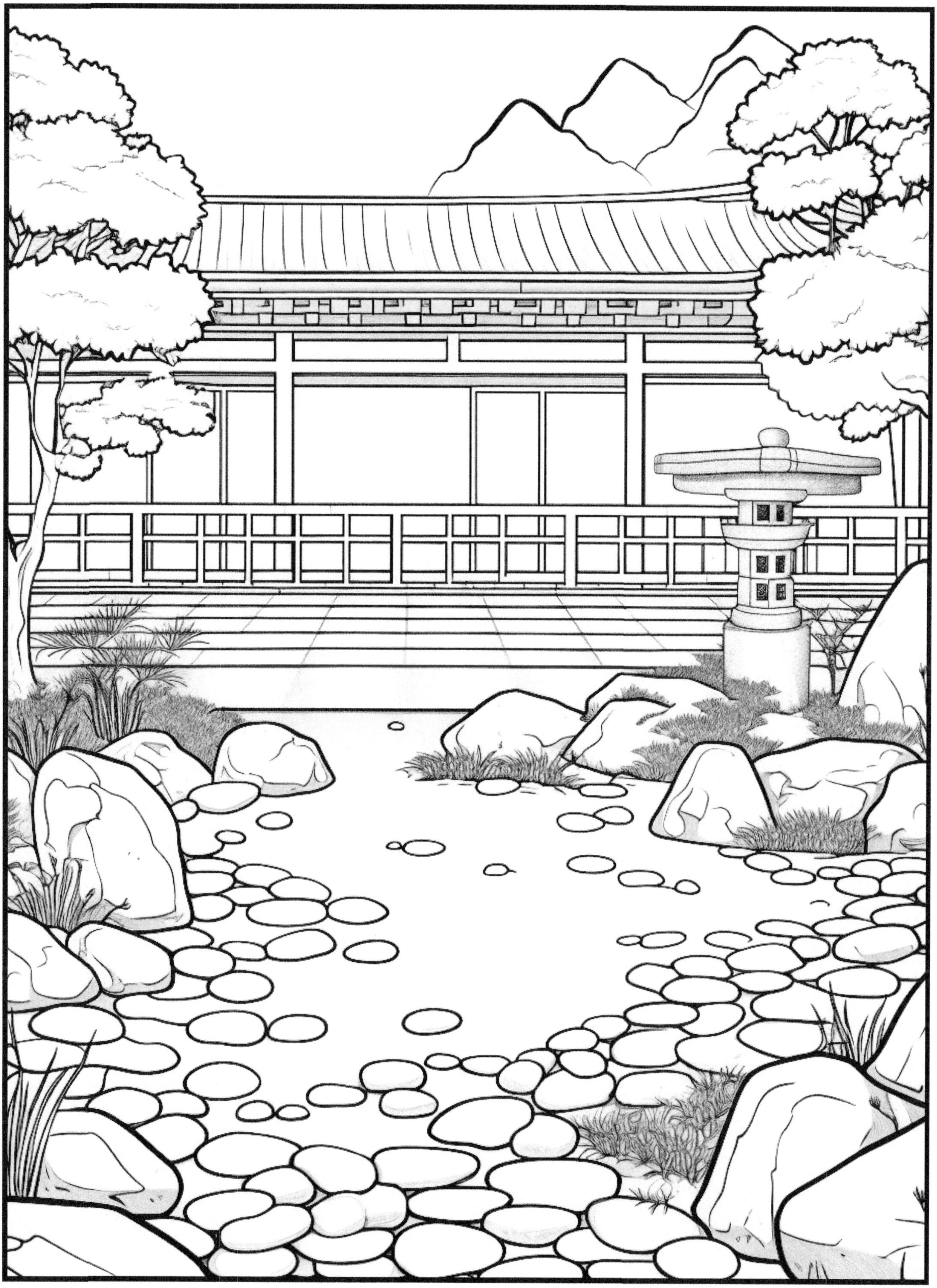

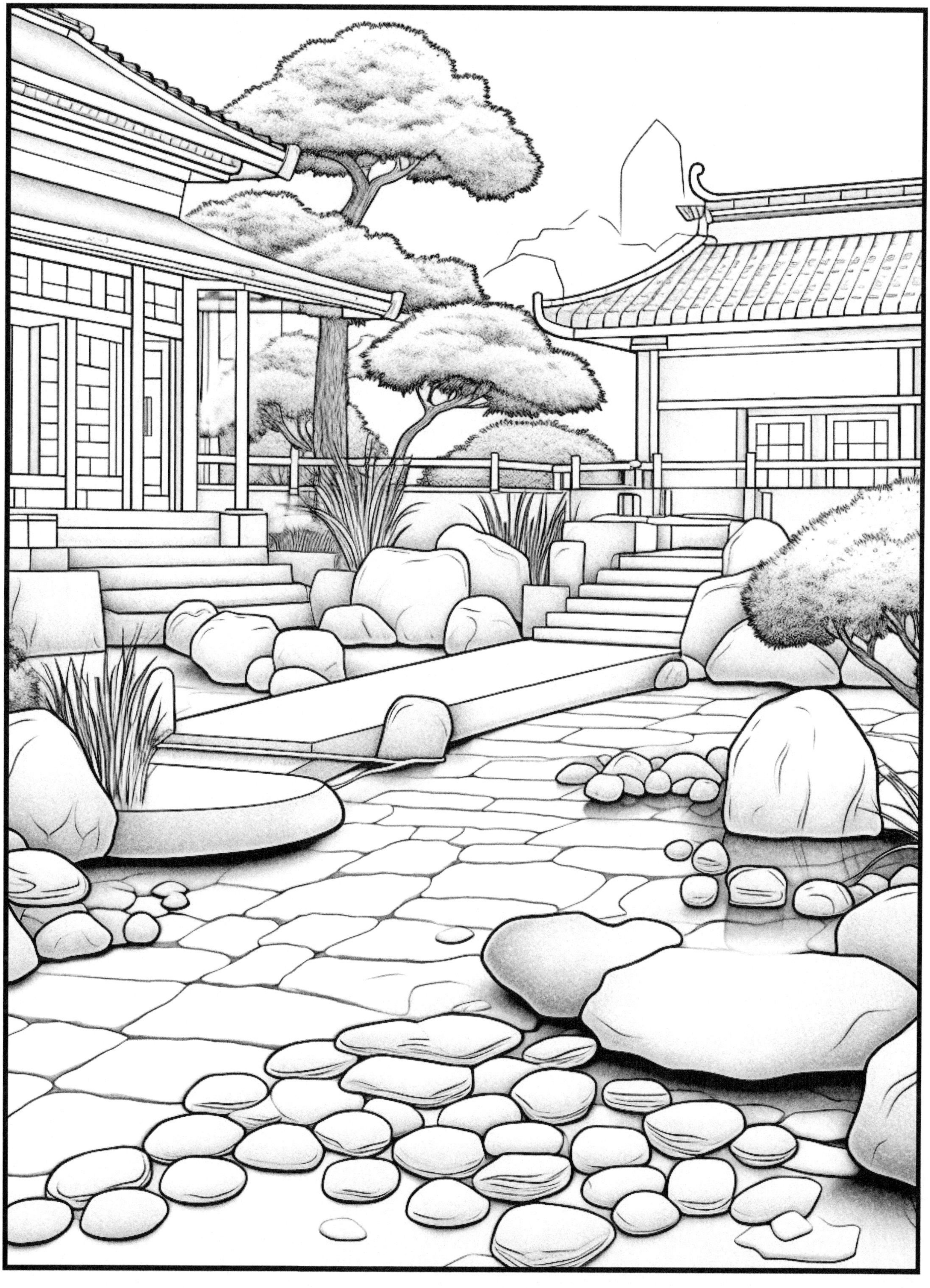

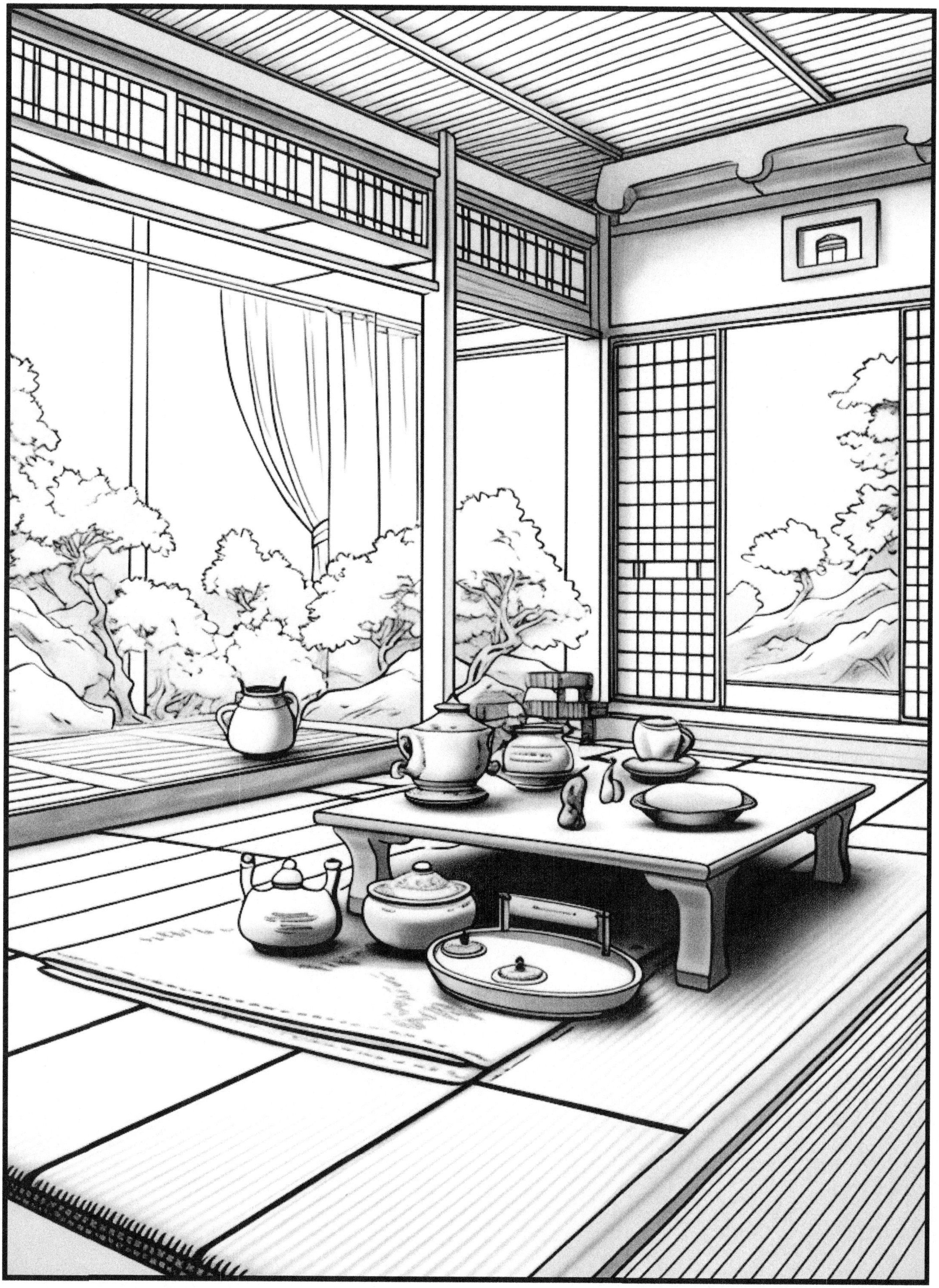

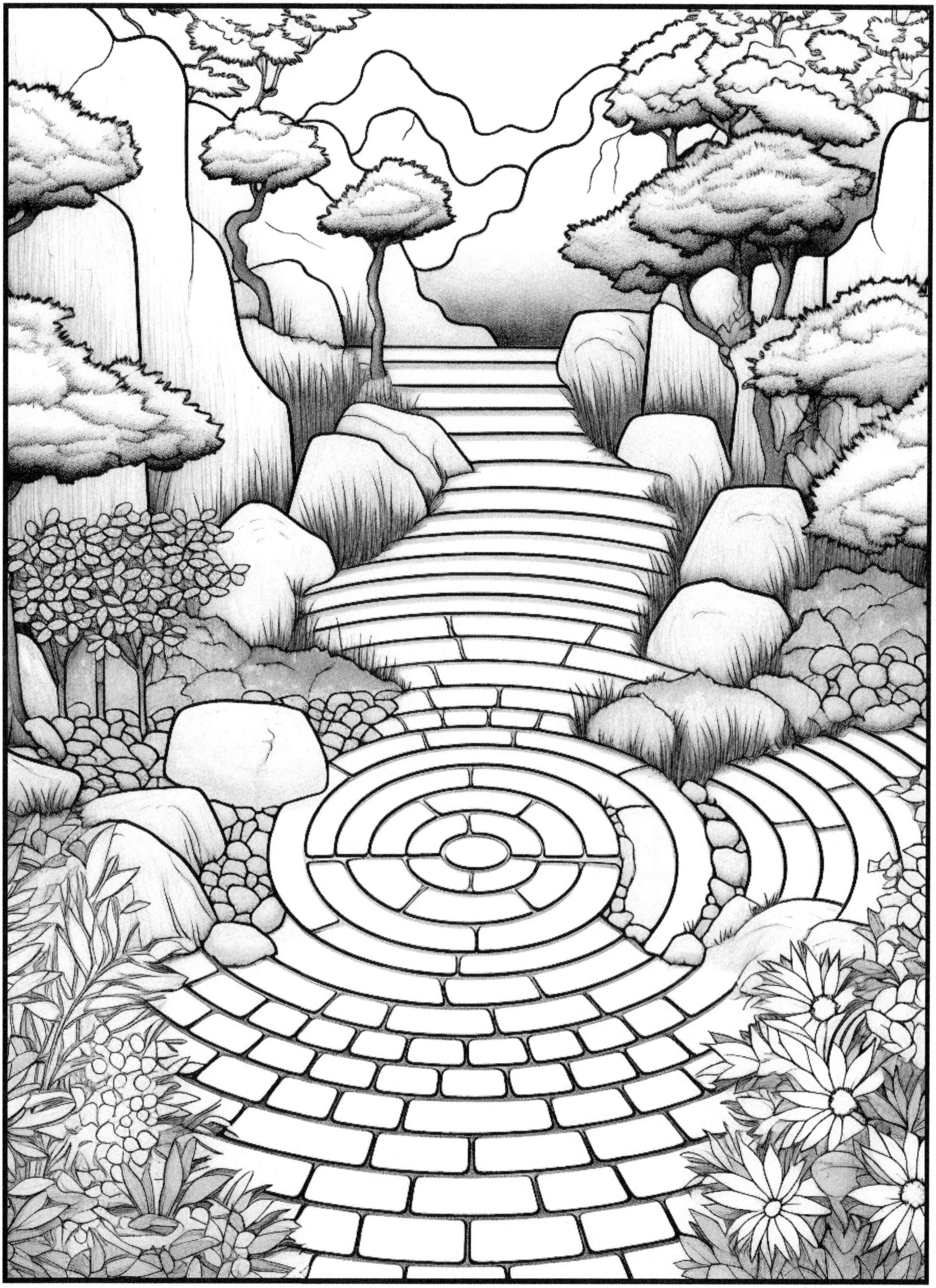

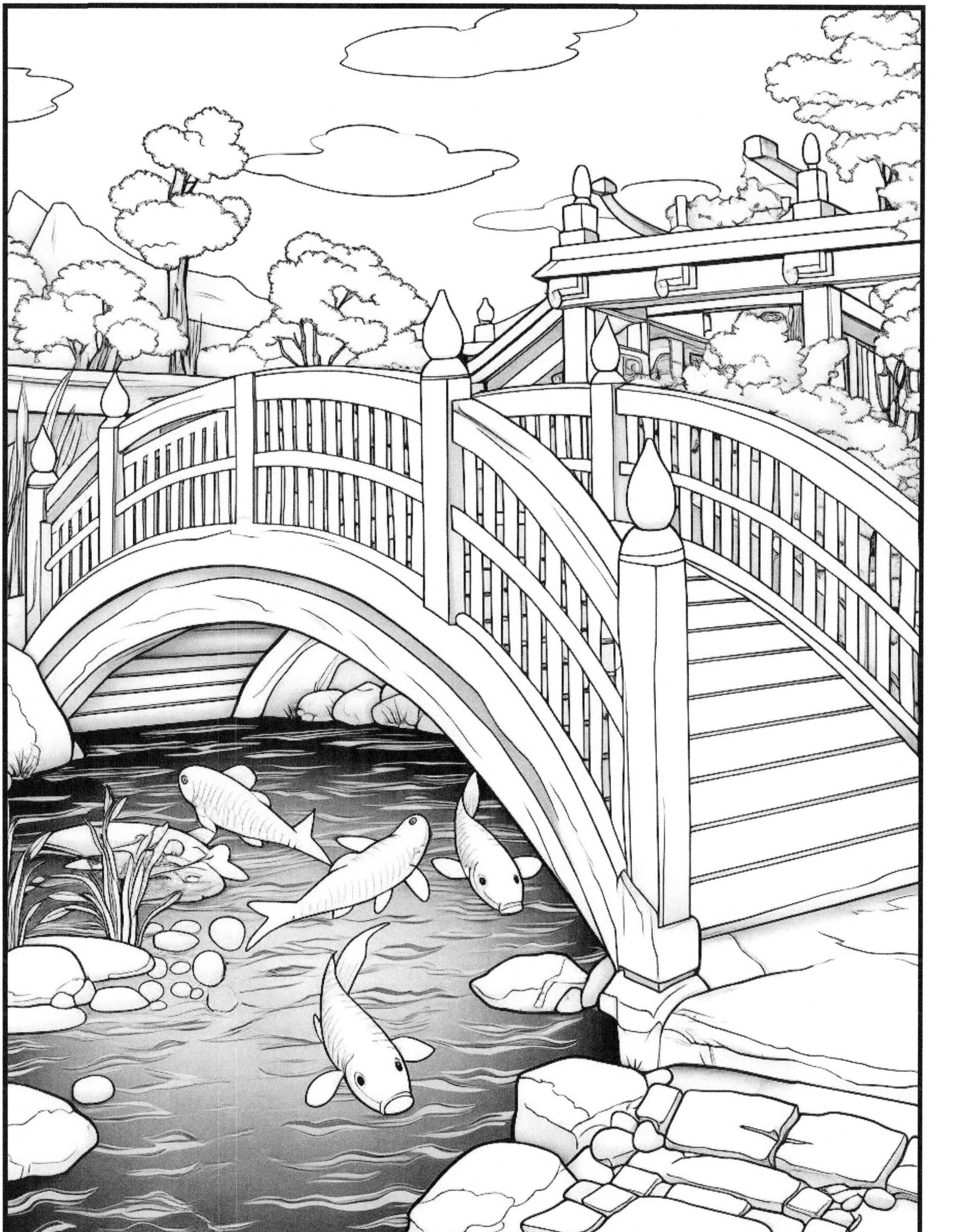

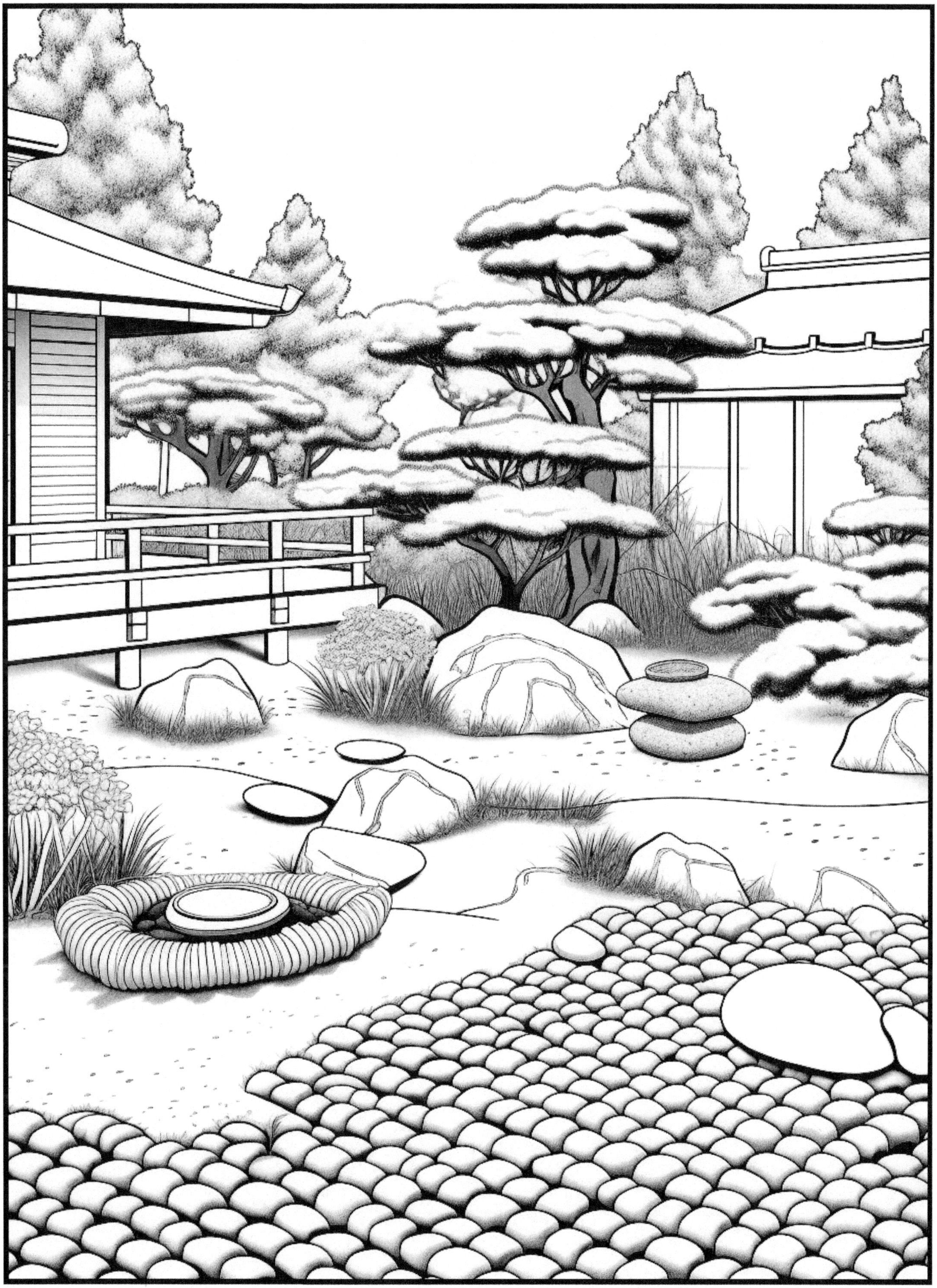

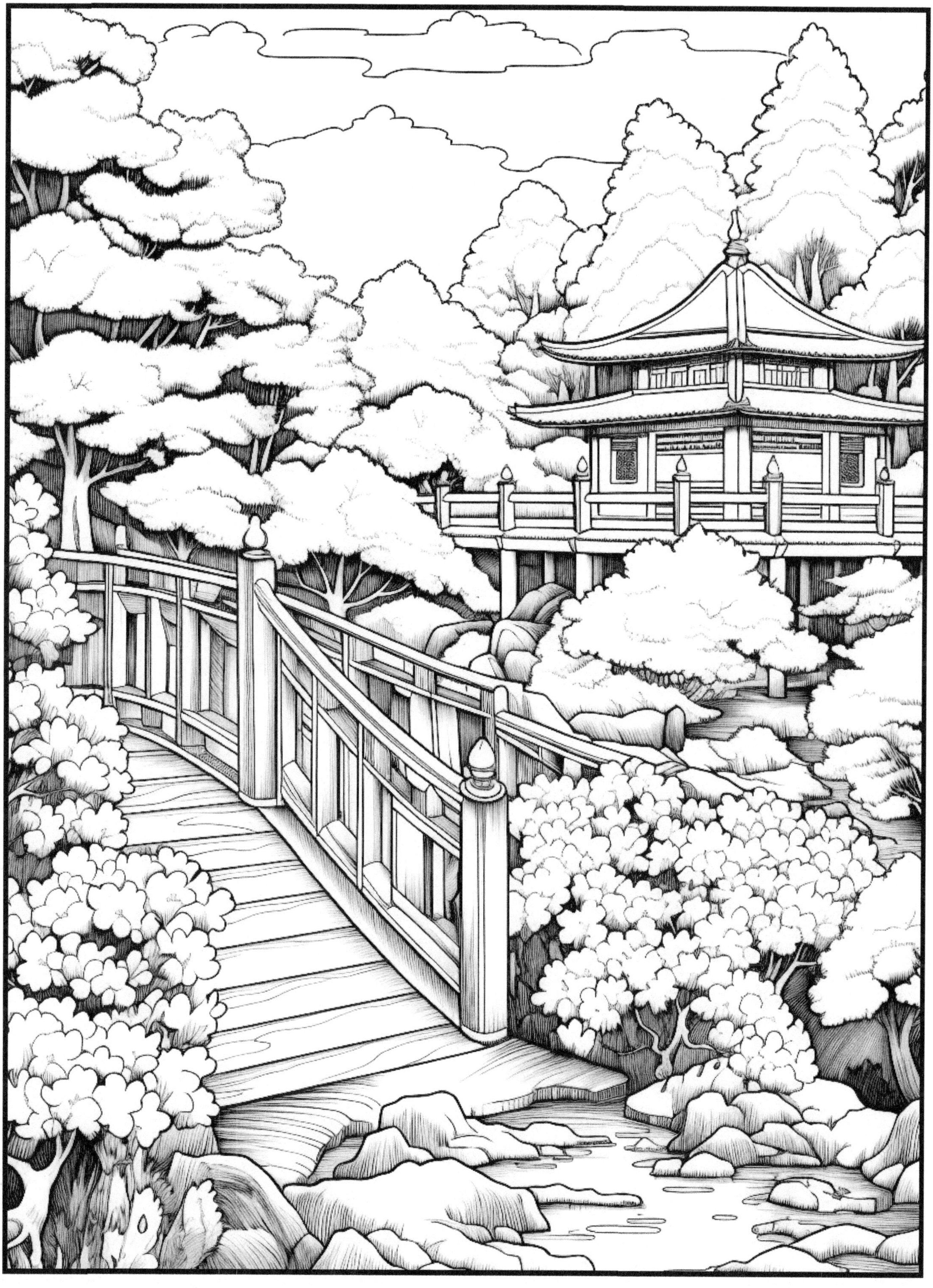

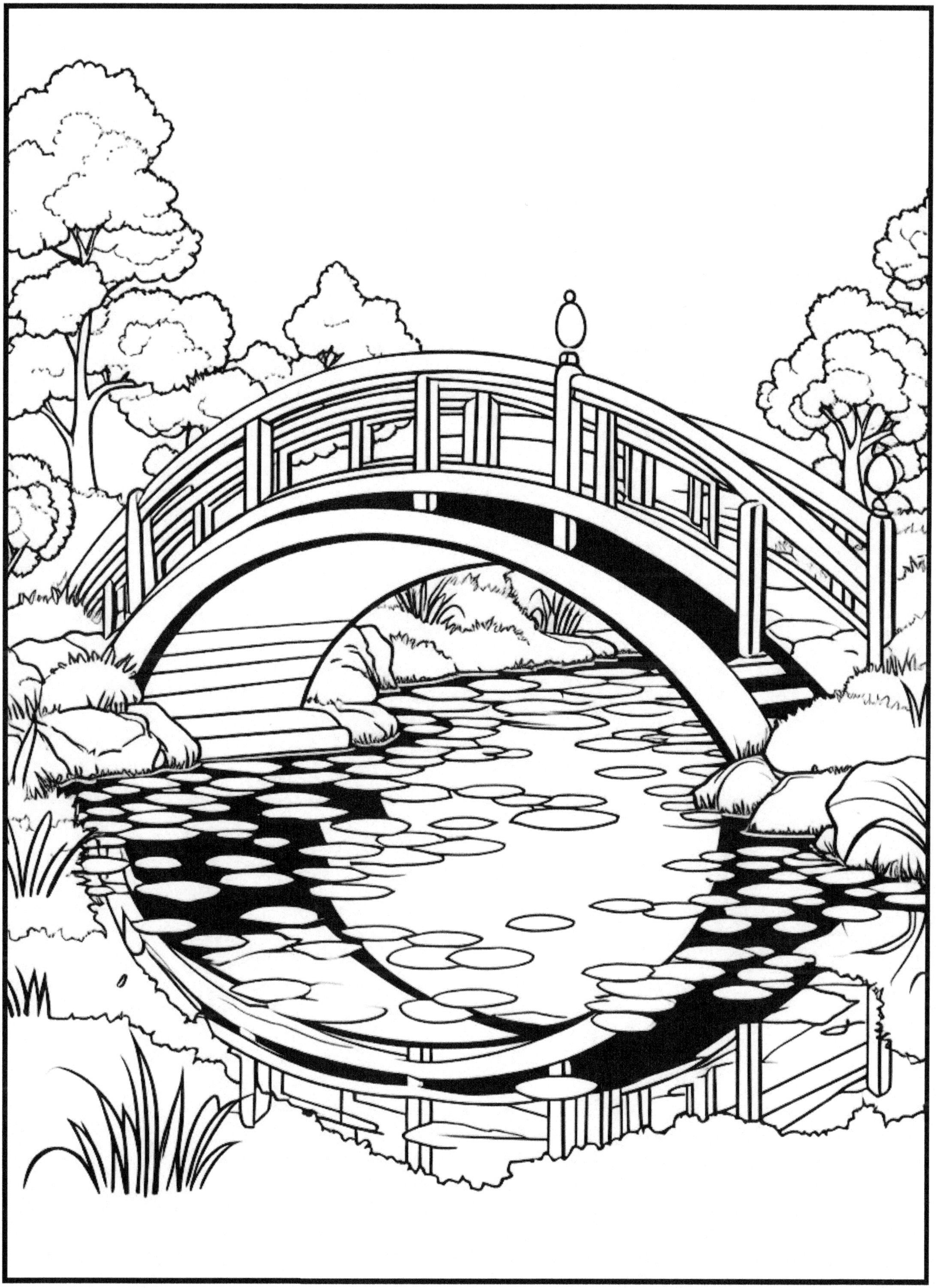

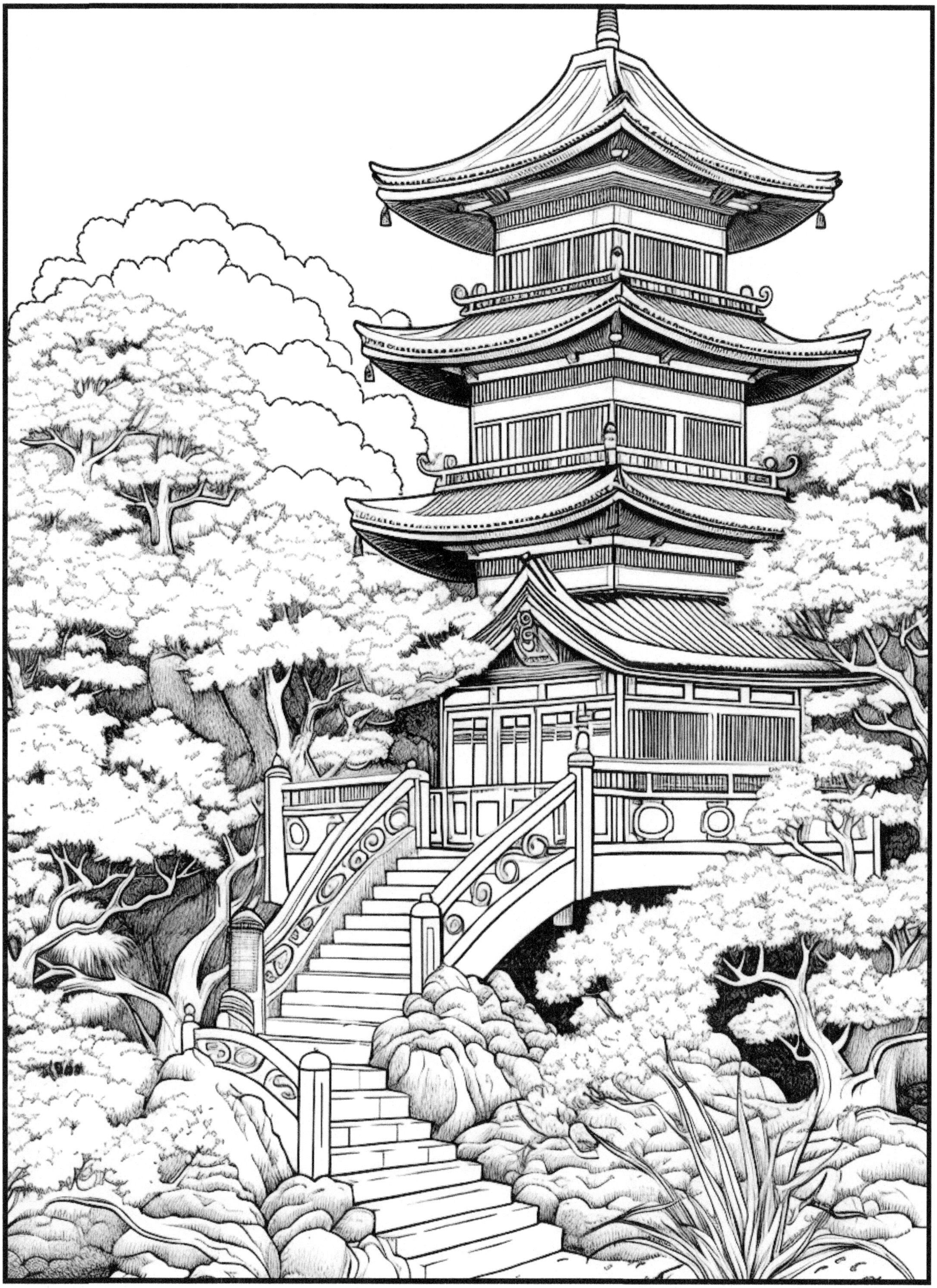

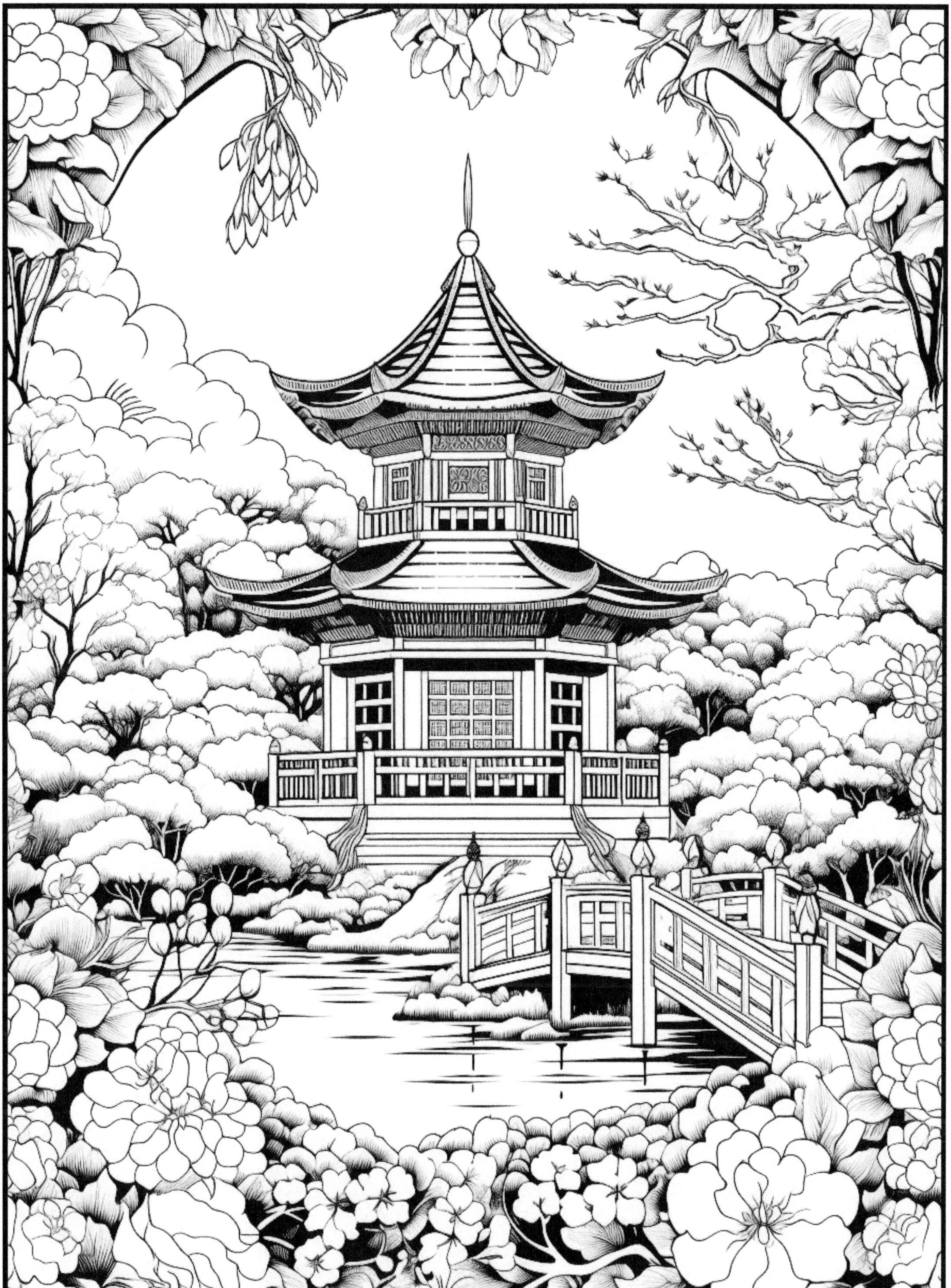

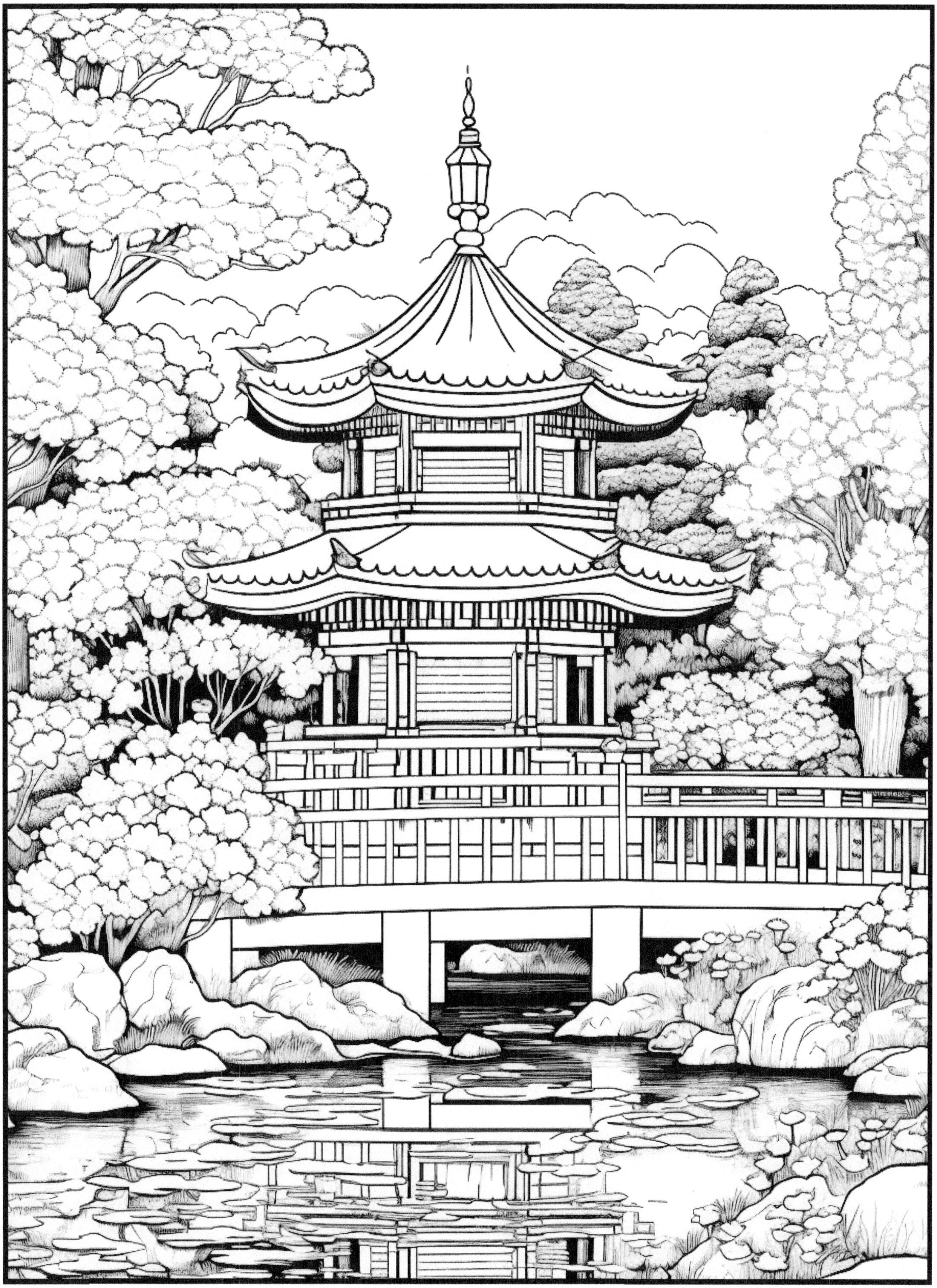

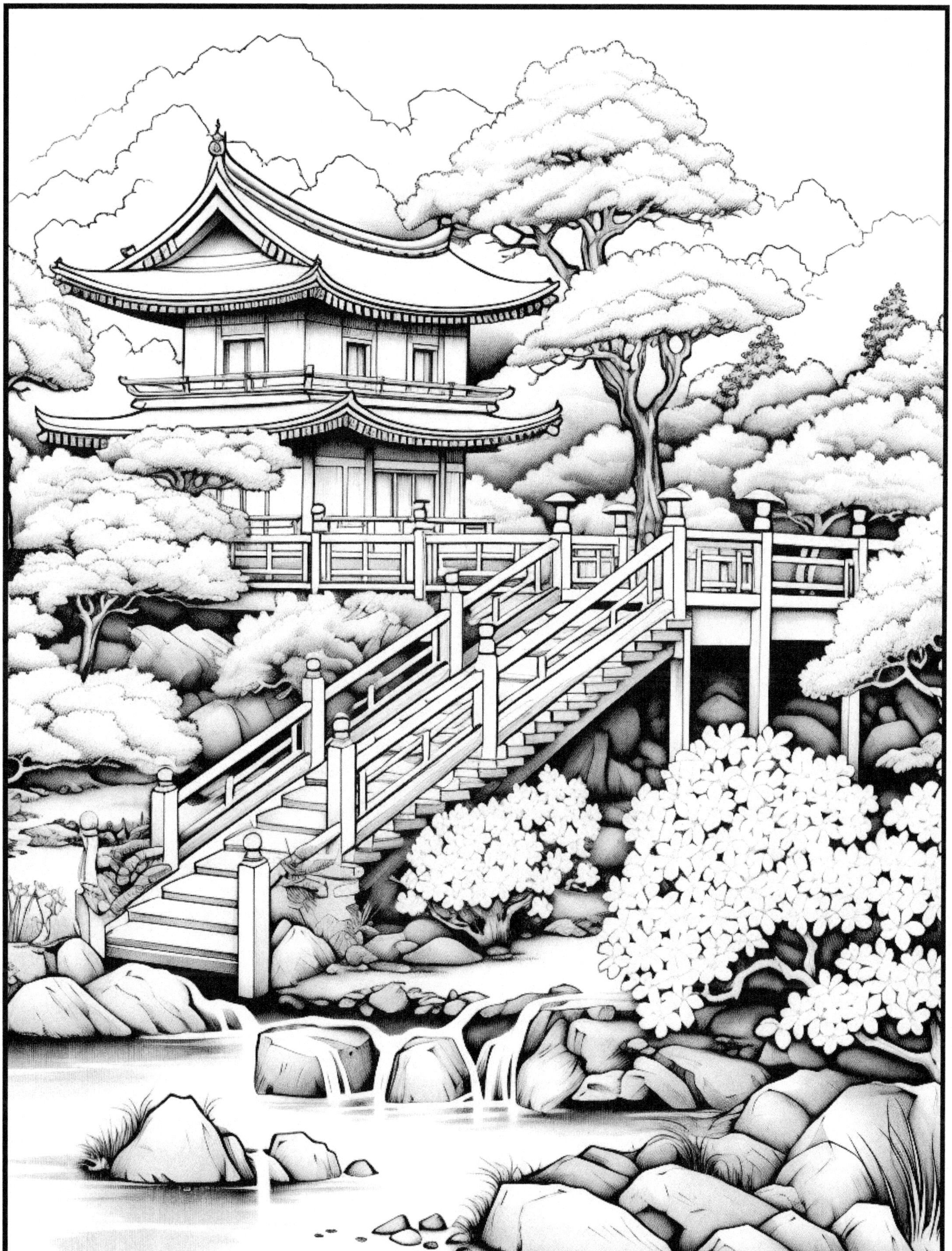

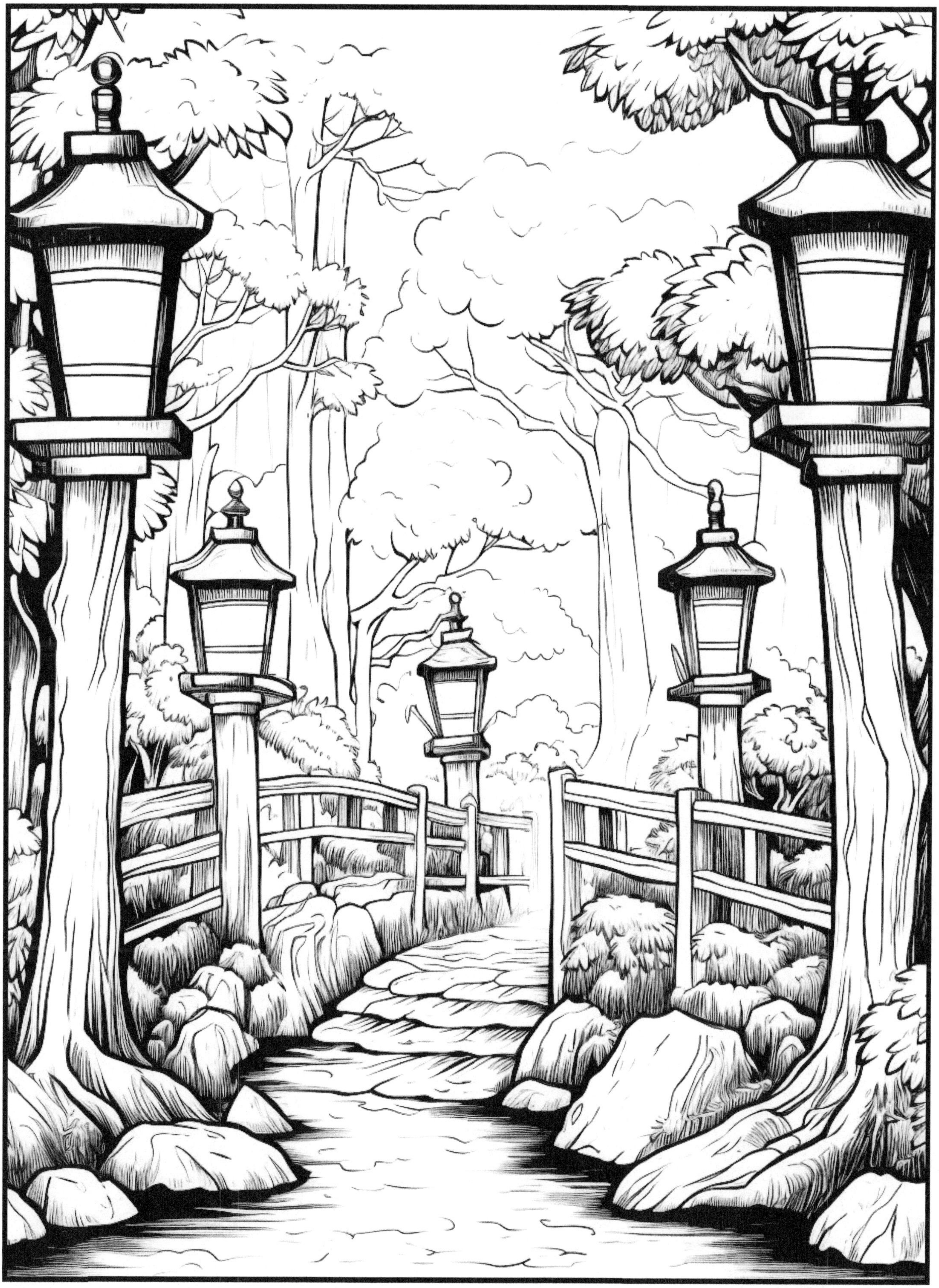

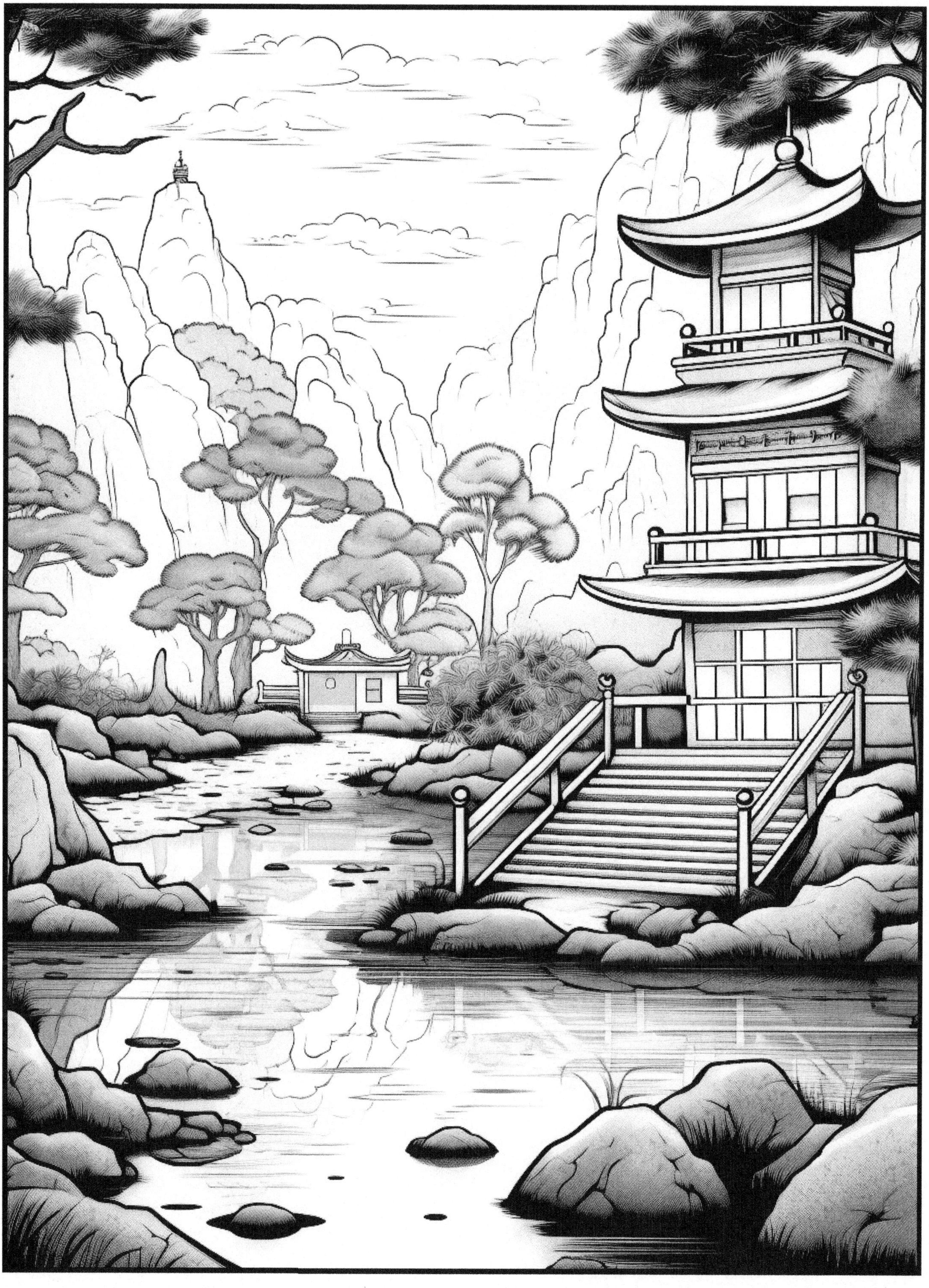

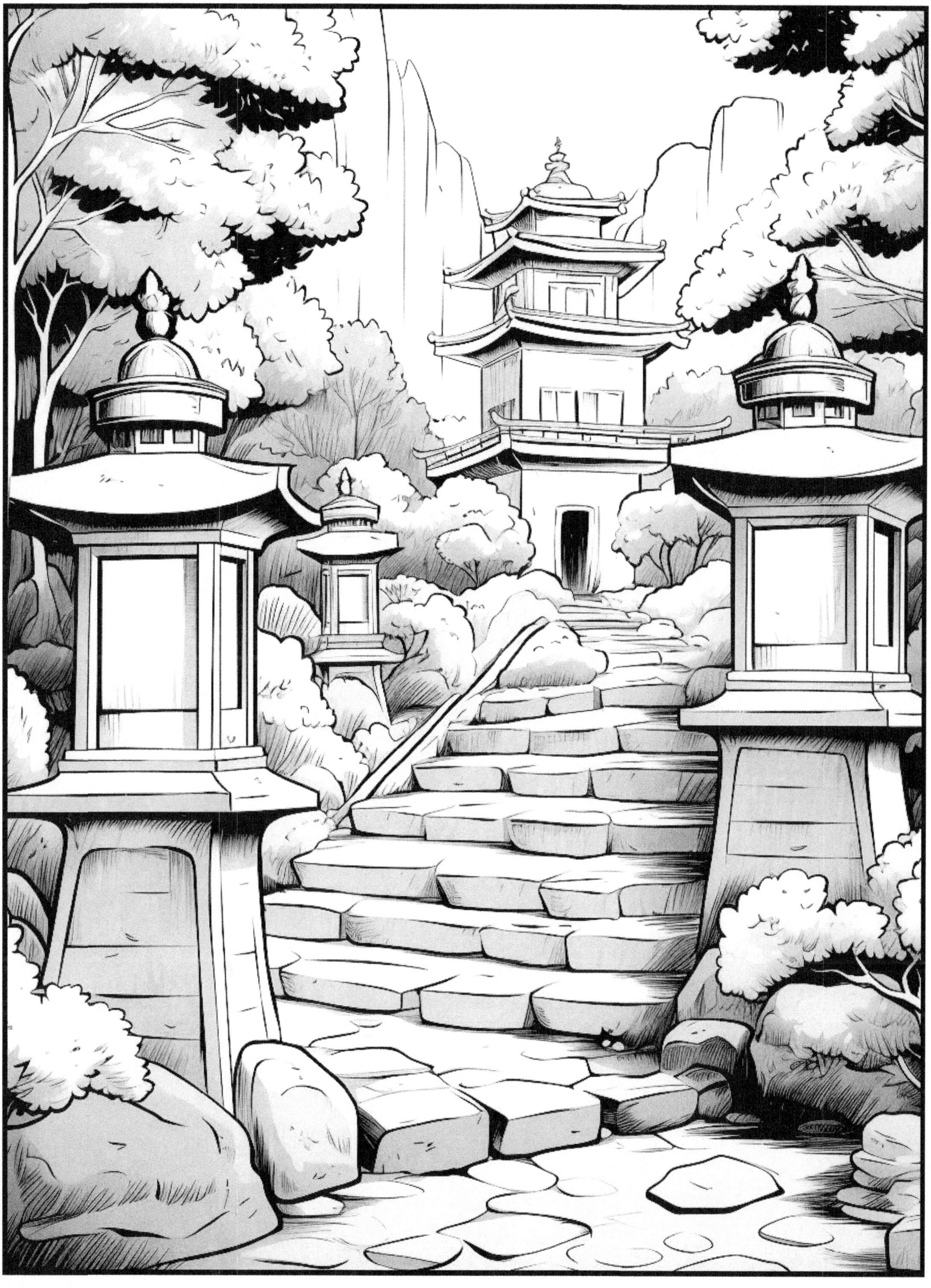

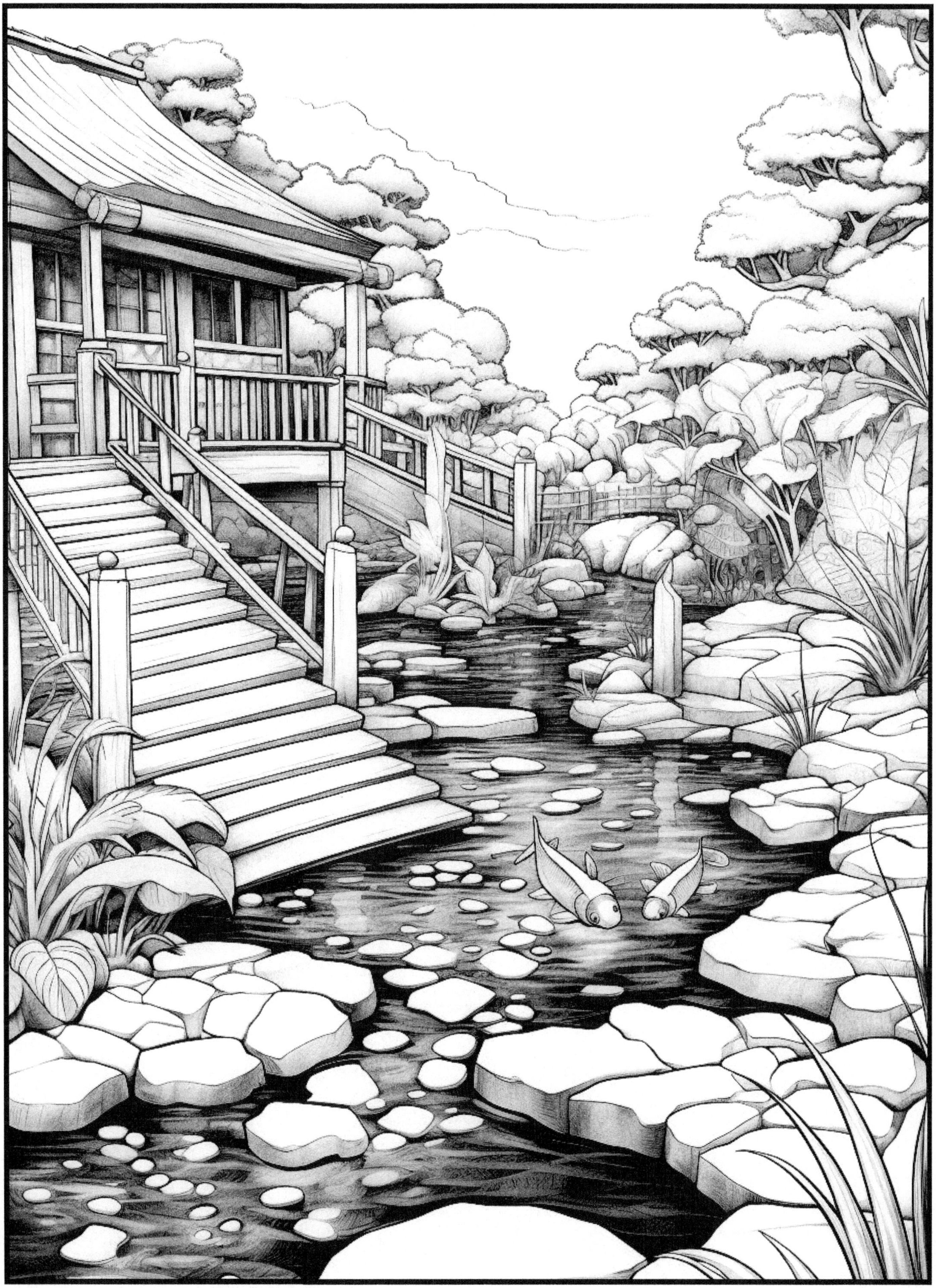

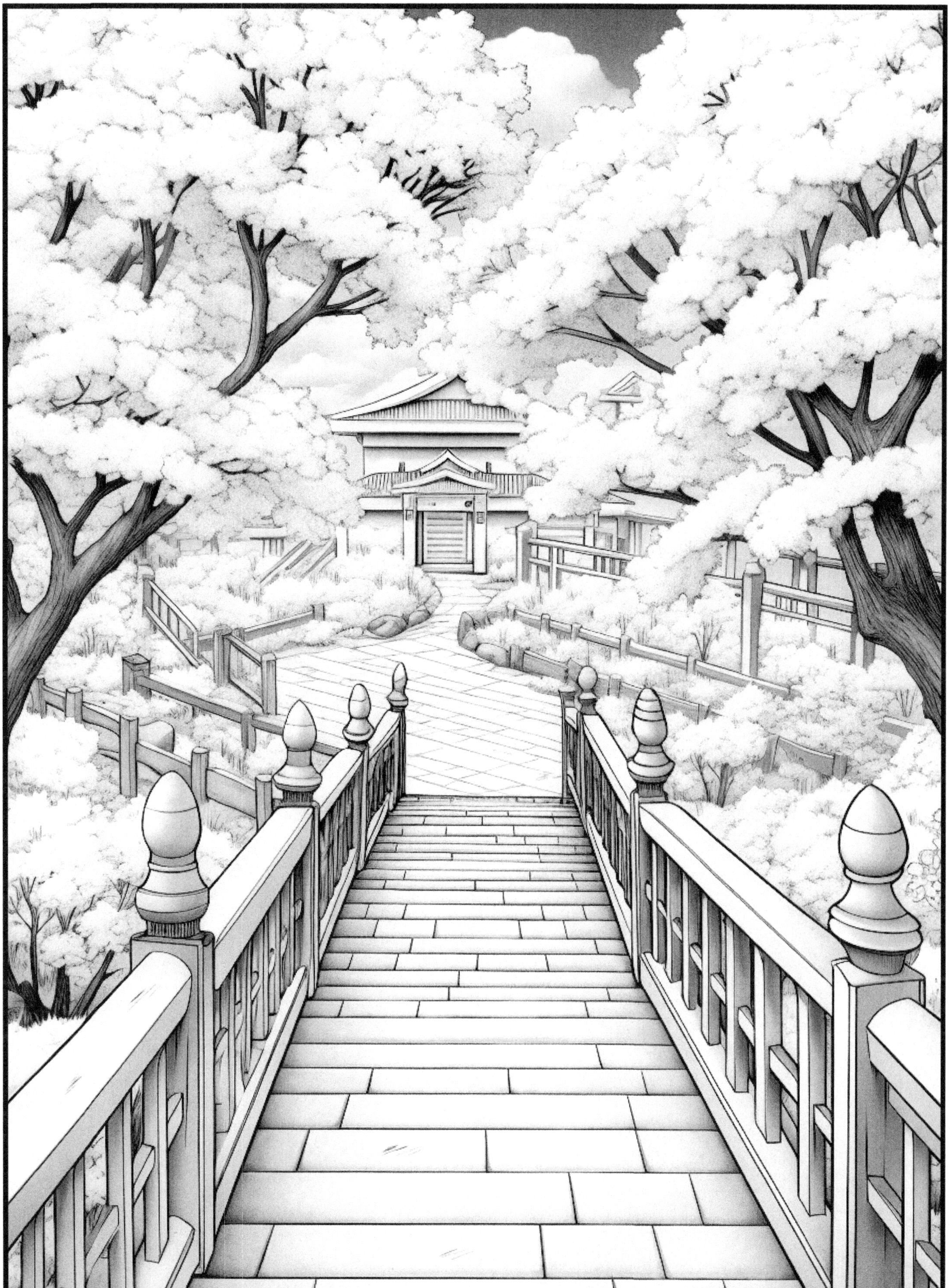

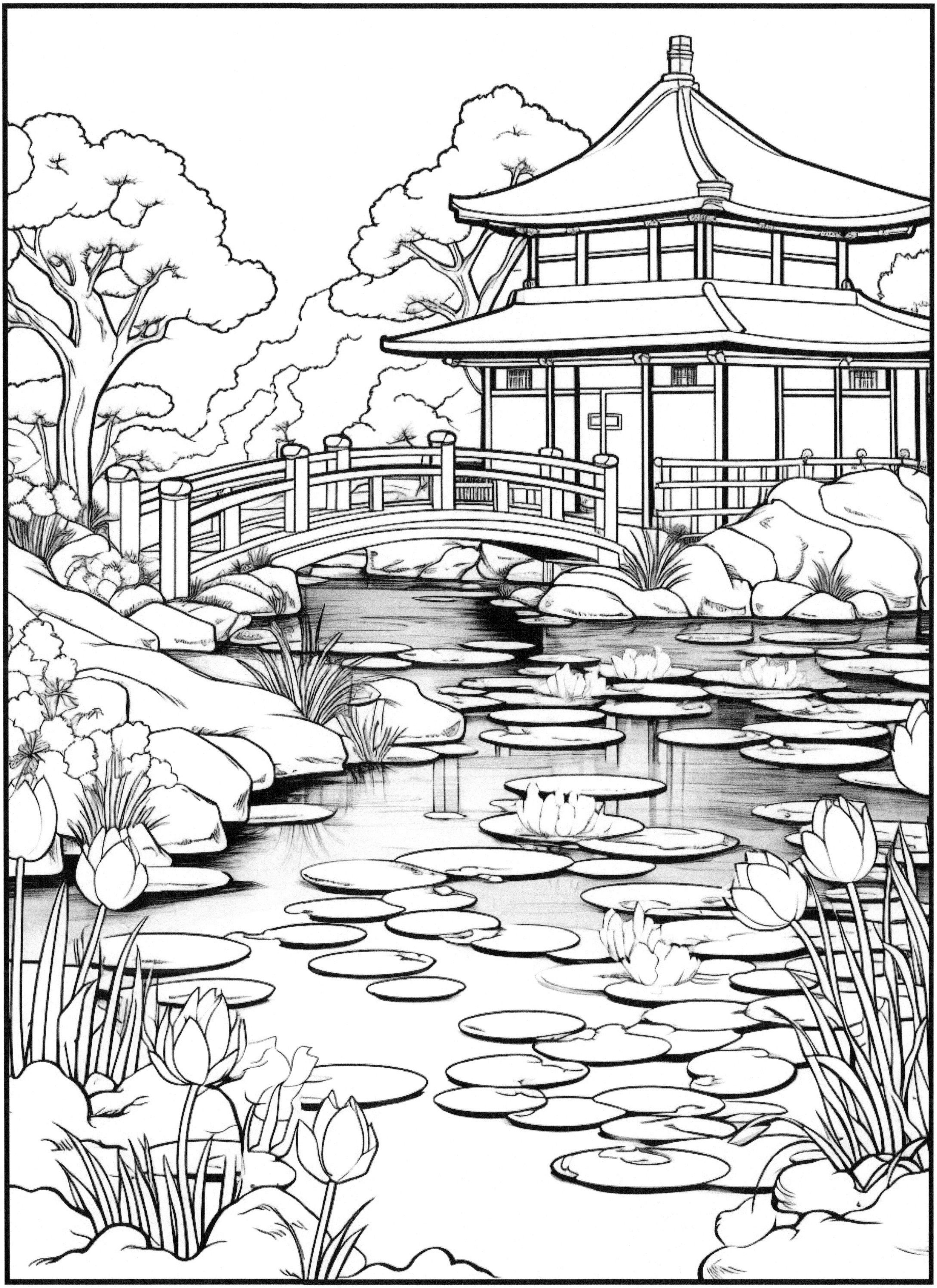

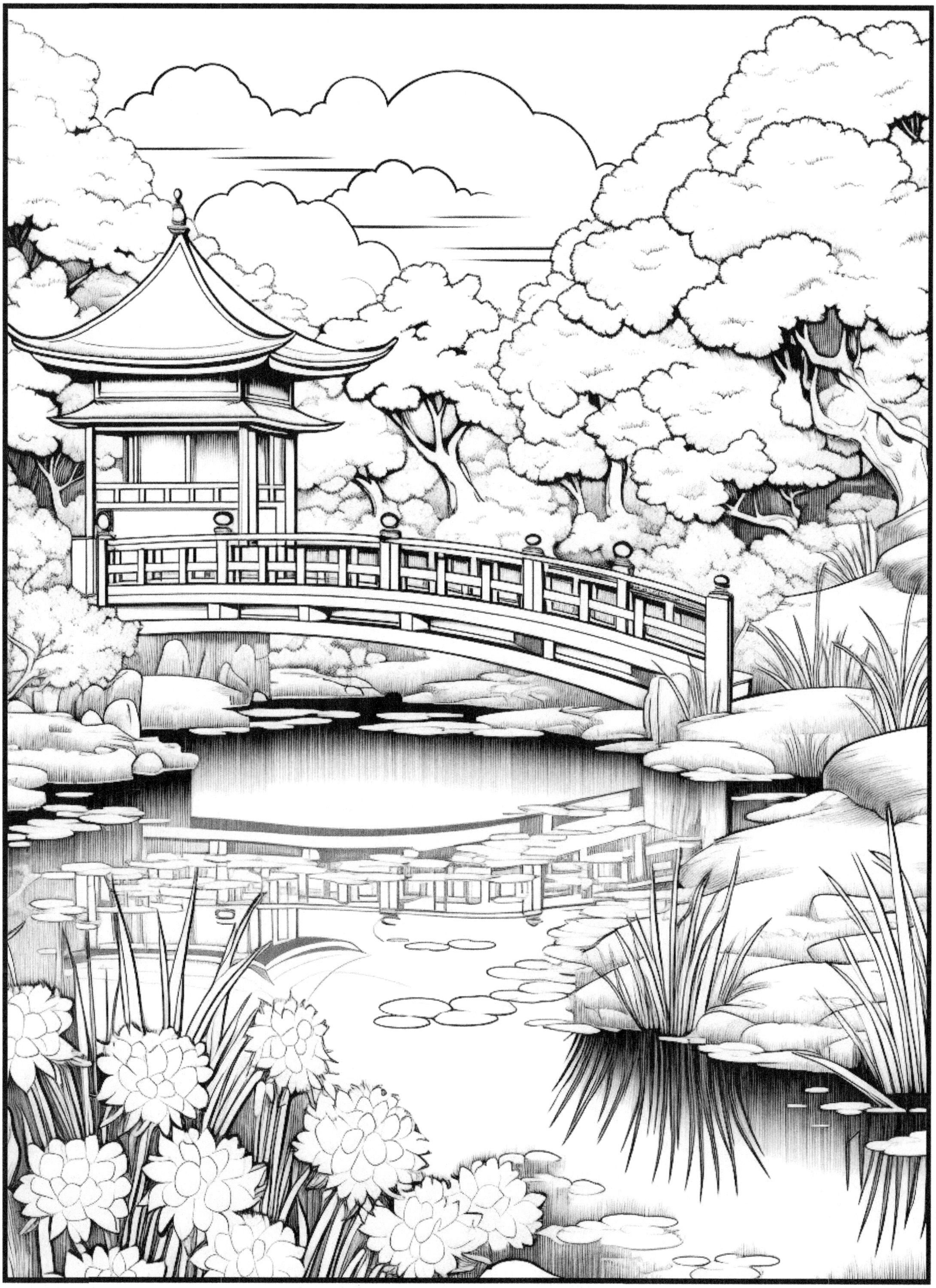

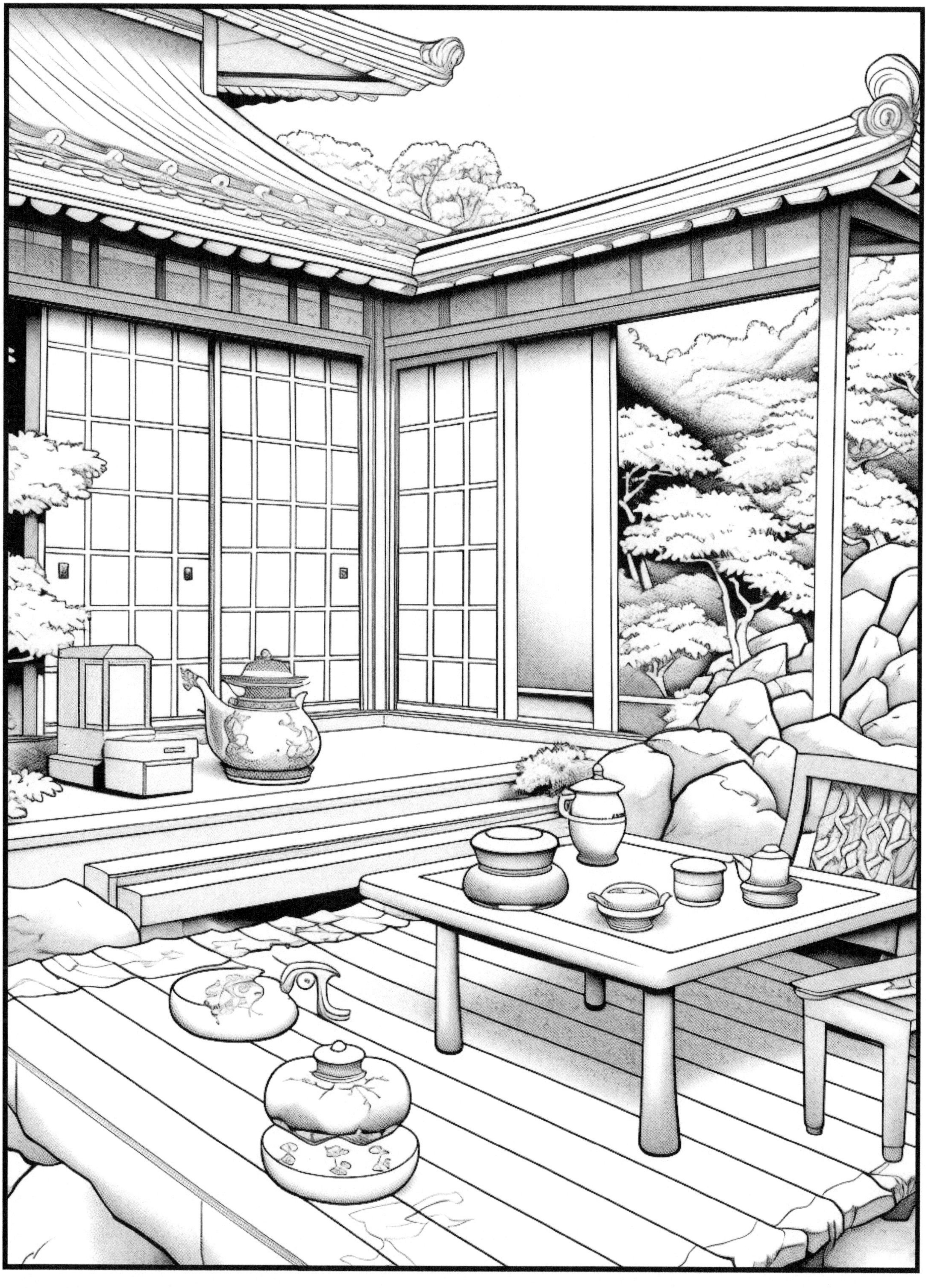

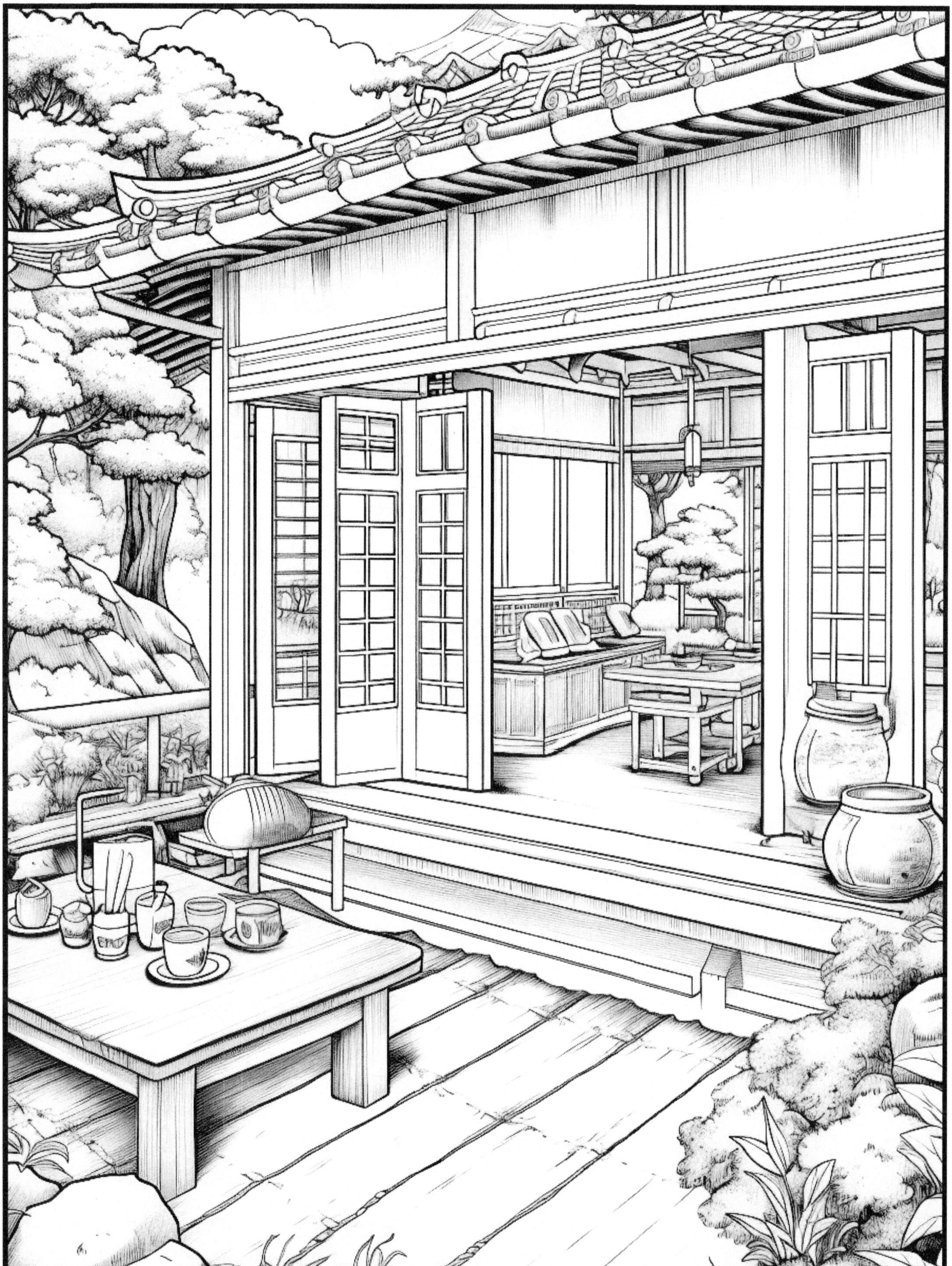

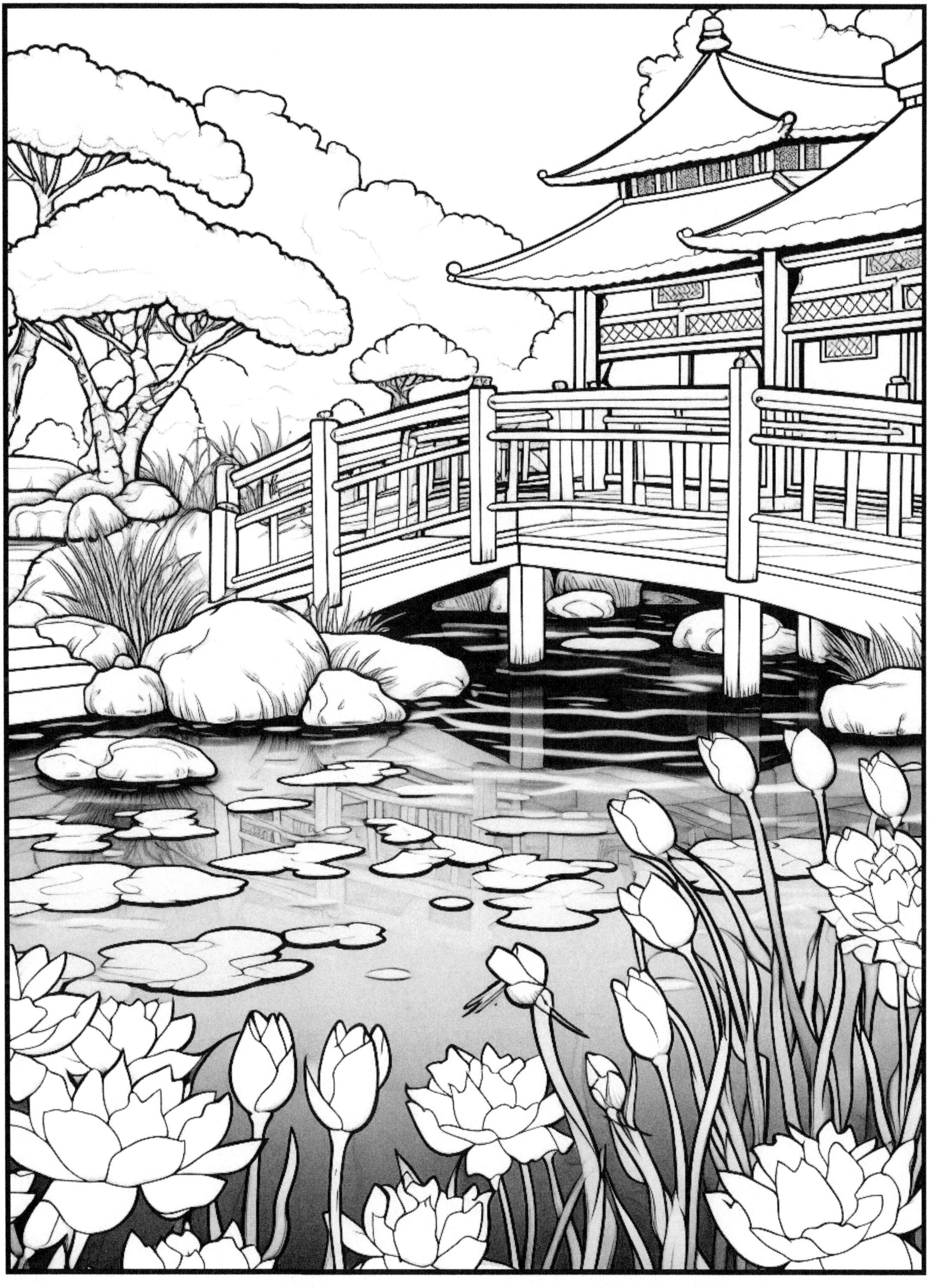

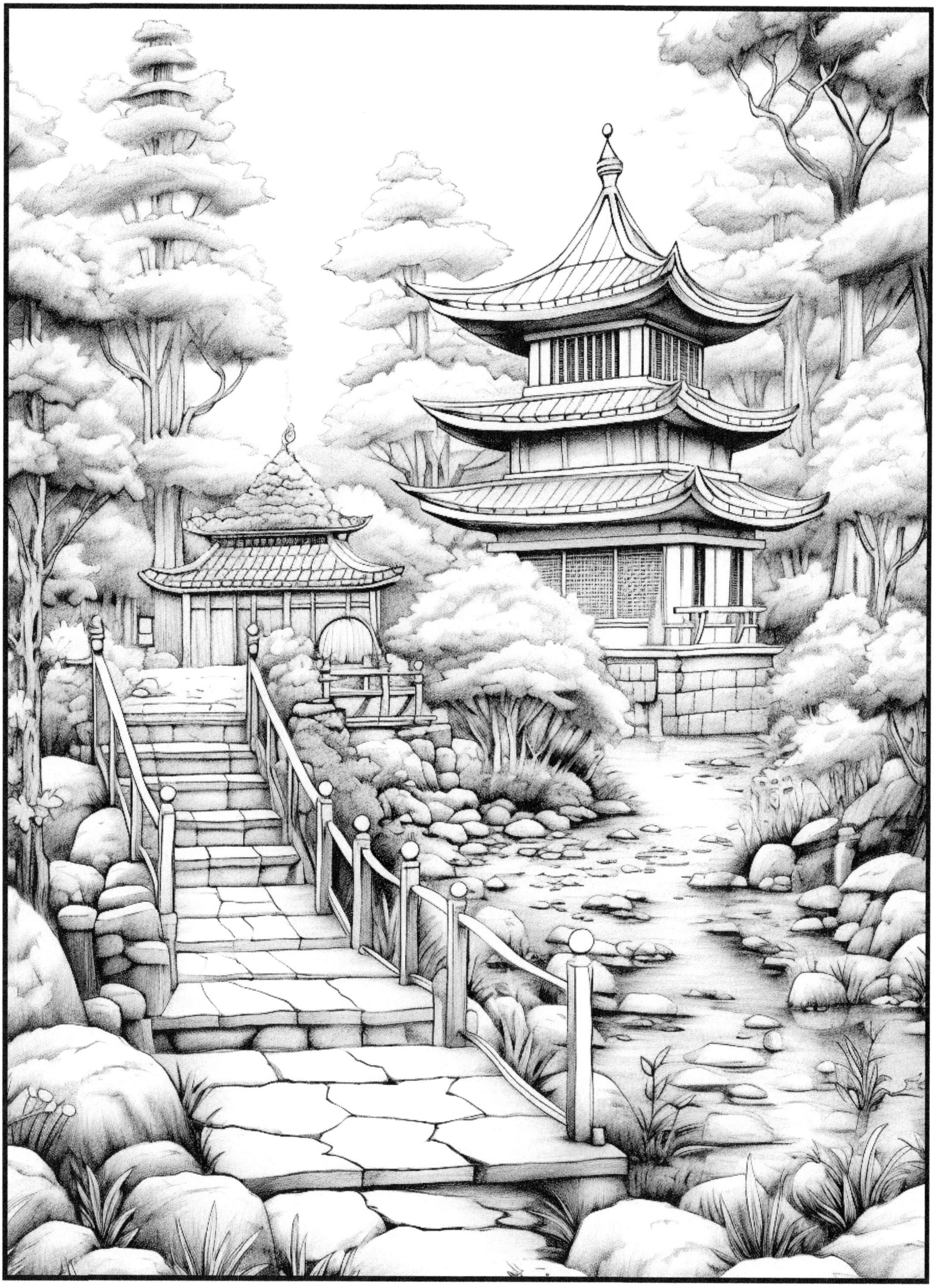

Printed in Great Britain
by Amazon